The Philosophical Psychology of William James

D1520799

Current Continental Research
is co-published by
The Center for Advanced Research
in Phenomenology
and
University Press of America, Inc.

CURRENT CONTINENTAL RESEARCH 005

Michael H. DeArmey & Stephen Skousgaard

editors

THE PHILOSOPHICAL PSYCHOLOGY OF WILLIAM JAMES

1986

Center for Advanced Research in Phenomenology
& University Press of America, Washington, D.C.

4720 Boston Way
Lanham, MD 20706

3 Henrietta Street
London WC2E 8LU England

Library of Congress Cataloging-in-Publication Data

The Philosophical psychology of William James.

   (Current continental research ; 005)
   Bibliography: p.
   Includes indexes.
   Contents: The place of William James's "Principles of
psychology" in American philosophy / Andrew J. Reck—
The anthropological foundations of William James's
philosophy / Michael H. DeArmey—The project of a
metaphysics of psychology in William James's "Principles
of psychology" / Lester Embree—[etc.]
   1. Psychology.   2. James William, 1842-1910.
Principles of psychology.   3. Phenomenological
psychology—Philosophy.   I. DeArmey, Michael H.,
1944-   .   II. Skousgaard, Stephen.   III. Series.
BF121.P47   1986   150   86-11024
ISBN 0-8191-5429-6 (alk. paper)
ISBN 0-8191-5430-X (pbk. : alk. paper)

CONTENTS

VIII

PREFACE

The not too distant future will witness the centennial celebration of the publication of William James's magnum opus, **The Principles of Psychology,** issued by Henry Holt and Company in 1890. The present volume contains seven essays which address the question of the fundamental nature of the thought contained in that great work. Thus, we hope that this collection will be studied not only for its intrinsic merits, but taken also as a call to reexamine all aspects of **The Principles of Psychology,** to assess past scholarship, and to engage thinkers everywhere in a discussion of the work's leading principles in light of subsequent developments over the last one hundred years.

James began **The Principles** in 1878, having contracted with Holt for a textbook in psychology. His marriage to Alice Howe Gibbens was to take place July 10, 1878, and he looked forward to a six to eight week honeymoon at the Putnam Camp, where, amidst the quiet majestic splendor of the Adirondack Mountains, he and his bride would enjoy the intimacy and freedom not obtainable in Cambridge or Boston. He arranged with Jim Putnam for exclusive use of the camp for that period, and in June, 1878, he wrote to Miss Gibbens from Keene Valley, New York: "I rec'd last night from Jim the formal offer of their cottage for the next 6 or 8 weeks. Hey diddle diddle! Isn't that good!"[1] But, true to his nature as a man permeated with the spirit of philosophic inquiry, he took with him to the Putnam shanty the books and materials necessary to begin his study of the principles of psychology. This work was thus commenced at a time of intense personal joy, and undoubtedly years later, when looking at the finished product fresh from the publisher, James's sense of achievement must have been infused with memories of that glorious summer. Upon receiving Francis J. Child's comments about mixing psychology with his honeymoon, James wrote back: "**She** (not Psyche but the bride) loves all these doctrines which are quite novel to her mind. . . She swears entirely by reflex action now, and believes in universal **Nothwendigkeit.**"[2] Summing up his summer honeymoon he told Child: "We have spent. . . a ballad-like summer in this delicious cot among the hills. We only needed crooks and a flock of sheet. I need not say that our psychic reaction has been one of content - perhaps as great as ever enjoyed by man."[3]

It was not until May of 1890 that James saw the end of the two-volume work in sight. On May 9th he wrote wearily to his publisher: "No one could be more disgusted than I at the sight of the book. **No** subject is worth being treated of in 1000 pages! . . . as it stands it is this or nothing -

a loathsome, distended, tumefied, bloated, dropsical mass, testifying to
nothing but two facts: **1st,** that there is no such thing as a **science** of
psychology, and **2nd,** that W. J. is an incapable."[4] Staying up late night
after night with the proofs, and fortifying himself with lots of coffee,
James recorded the great event: at 9:50 p.m. Sunday night, May 18, 1890 -
"The job is done!"[5] Having sent it off once and for all to the publisher,
James sunk into a dream-like numbness, envisioning at last a future of
"reading and living and loving out from the shadow of that interminable
black cloud,"[6] every page of which had been written "four or five times"[7]
and every sentence of which had to be forged "in the teeth of irreducible
and stubborn facts" as well as meeting "the resistence of other philosophers."[8] Rested, his estimate of his achievements was that he had produced "a vigorous and richly colored chunk," that as "'Psychologies' go,
it is a good one," that it has assisted in the task of making psychology a
natural science, and that it would contribute to making the year 1890 "a
memorable one in American literature. . ."[9]. These judgments are eminently
reasonable, although James did not perhaps realize the permanent contribution he had made to Western thought. He worried that **The Principles** and
other psychological works of his generation might be surpassed by more
scientific ones, leaving them "to become unreadable old medieval
lumber."[10] As the bibliography and essays included in this volume show,
worry was mistaken at least with respect to his own work.

A rough summation of the history of the impact of **The Principles of
Psychology** would distinguish two chief periods. In the first and earlier
period many thinkers were captivated by the book's naturalism. By
'natualism' I mean to capture those descriptions of James's psychology
that dominated the literature from 1890 to the early 1940s. **The Principles**
was variously described as biological, naturalistic, cerebral, evolutionary, medical, positivistic, functional, or behavioristic. The second
period, from about 1942 to the present, is marked by the rise of the
Continental interpretation of James's psychology, an interpretation initiated by phenomenologists such as Alfred Schutz and Aron Gurwitsch, and
still continuing to provide a rich harvest of phenomenological insight.
The essays in this volume reflect the preoccupations of both periods and
address most of the basic questions that can be asked in regard to **The
Principles.**

In anticipation of the centennial of 1990, I wish to add two suggestions as to what might still be done to improve our understanding of
The Principles. First and foremost, a genuine commentary is needed. By
this I do not mean a study of **The Principles** with the primary end in view

of establishing James as a member of some tradition or movement. I mean, rather, an historical-critical study which would investigate the sources he used - what he selected, rejected, modified, and why. Many of James's ideas were worked out by interacting with members of clubs or societies. The most famous instance of this is the Metaphysical Club of the early 1870s, the impact of which shows up clearly in James's 1878 article on Spencer, which forshadows pragmatism. Lesser known are James's activities in the same club in the late 1870s, when it was revived by that hot-blooded Scotsman, Thomas Davidson. Another instance would be James's interaction with Hodgson and other members of the Aristotelian Society in 1879-1880. Many of James's ideas about space, time, the a priori, relations, and subject/object were developed at the latter two clubs. We need also to know more about James's relation to the physiologists, particularly those close at hand - James J. Putnam and Henry Bowditch. While some of this scholarship has been accomplished, it is scattered far and wide and needs consolidation, comparison, and evaluation in a commentary.

Another lacuna is the study of James's style in **The Principles,** his choice of argumentive form, his use of illustrations and metaphor, his adaptation of literary expressions, and whether this style has 'ontological significance.' James's style was the single most widely discussed aspect of **The Principles** when it first appeared. James Sully, in his review in **Mind,** complained of the "dazzling effect" of James's style, in particular the "rollicking defiance of the authorities."[11] Peirce accused James of "idiosyncracies of diction and tricks of language such as usually spring up in households of great talent."[12] G. Stanley Hall chose to describe James as an "impressionist in psychology," whose portfolio contains some sketches "equisite and charming in detail," others rough in outline, the whole thing a bundle of inconsistencies and incoherencies reflecting the unrest of the times.[13] George Santayana defended James's style. It functioned as "a safe-guard against pretension and hollowness" so often found in those thinkers with the architechtonic instinct. The "cold breath" of these thinkers of symmetry, balance, and precision

> . . . congeals the surface of truth into some system; and on that thin ice they glide merrily over allthe chasms in their knowledge. But Professor James's simplicity and genuineness have saved him from this danger. He is eager for discovery. . . it would be pedantry to regret the loss of logical unity in a book so rich and living, in which a generous nature breaks out at every point, and the perennial

problems of the human mind are discussed so modestly, so solidly, with such a deep and pathetic sincerity.[14]

If we take this interpretation seriously, then we must consider the possibility that James adopted a style of composition for **The Principles** which would grope for systematization but simultaneously and deliberately push into colorful relief the gaps in human knowlege. This is Jacques Barzun's view: ". . . James's style is the perfect mirror of his philosophy, where 'what really **exists** is not things made, but things in the making.'"[15] In reply to Ward's criticism that he was not systematic enough, James replied: "Yes, I am too systematic and loose! but in this case I permited myself to remain so deliberately, on account of the strong aversion with which I am filled for the humbugging pretense of exactitude. . . that has prevailed in psychological literature."[16] **The Principles**, as Perry puts it, "was read because it was readable. . . the reader constantly recognized himself in its descriptions and illustrations."[17]

This volume derives from a double session of the Society for the History of Philosophy, meeting with the American Philosophical Association, in December 1982. That double session was organized by Lester Embree of Duquesne University and devoted to The Philosophical Significance of **The Principles of Psychology** of William James. Subsequently, Dr. Stephen Skousgaard and I became the editors. We were guided in our efforts by Professor Embree and take this opportunity to express our gratitude to him. Funding for research, typing, editorial assistance, etc. came from the University of Southern Mississippi. The editors wish to thank Dr. Karen Yarborough, Vice-President of Research at the University of Southern Mississippi, for her support of this project. We also wish to thank Carleigh Scates, Sherry Braswell, and Normia Davis for their many hours of work in facilitating the appearance of this book.

Michael H. DeArmey
The University of Southern Mississippi

NOTES

1. Undated letter, William James Papers, Houghton Library, Harvard University. Quoted by permission.

2. **The Letters of William James,** Henry James III editor. Boston: Little, Brown, and Company, 1926, 196.

3. **Ibid.**, 197.

4. **Ibid.**, 294.

5. **Ibid.**, 295.

6. **Ibid.**

7. **Ibid.**, 297.

8. Quoted in Ralph Barton Perry, **The Thought and Character of William James.** 2 vols.: Boston and Toronto: Little, Brown and Company, 1935, II, 40. Hereafter cited as "TC."

9. **Letters,** 294-7.

10. **Letters,** 296.

11. Quoted in TC, II, 104.

12. Quoted in TC, II, 104-105.

13. Quoted in TC, II, 108-109.

14. Quoted in TC, II, 110-111.

15. Jacques Barzun, "William James, Author," **The American Scholar,** 52 (Winter, 1982/83), 46.

16. TC, II, 96.

17. TC, II, 91.

ESSAY ONE

THE PLACE OF WILLIAM JAMES'S "PRINCIPLES OF PSYCHOLOGY" IN AMERICAN PHILOSOPHY

Andrew J. Reck
Tulane University

In the Preface to the series of papers on William James's **Principles of Psychology** presented as part of the program of the American Psychological Association's Seventy-Fifth Anniversary Convention, it is declared: "James's **Principles** is without question the most literate, the most provocative, and at the same time the most intelligible book in psychology that has ever appeared in English or in any other language."[1] Although it would be extravagant to make a similar claim for the place of this work in philosophy, I believe it may be soberly asserted that it is the greatest book authored by an American philosopher. The significance of a work in philosophy is to be measured by the lasting importance of the problems with which it deals and by the stimuli its treatment of these problems, palpable not only in coherence but in suggestiveness, provides for acceptance or for further inquiry. By these criteria of significance James's **Principles of Psychology** is undoubtedly the greatest single work in American philosophical literature.

The capacity of James's **Principles** to inspire philosophers of diverse temperaments was evident from its first appearance; it has recently been reactivated in the abundant and ever-growing commentaries on the American philosopher-psychologist. Original thinkers as well as philosophical scholars have drawn nourishment from this book. Edmund Husserl, Alfred North

The **Philosophical Psychology of William James**, edd. Michael H. DeArmey & Stephen Skousgaard, Copyright 1986, The Center for Advanced Research in Phenomenology, Inc. and co-published by arrangement with The University Press of America, Inc., Washington, D.C., U.S.A.

1

Whitehead, and Ludwig Wittgenstein, - three non-pragmatist thinkers of the
first rank in our century - have borrowed from James's **Principles.** No
wonder Whitehead once compared James to Descartes and attributed to the
American philosopher-psychologist "the inauguration of a new stage in
philosophy."[2]

The existentialist and phenomenological tendencies in James's **Princi-
ples** have attracted a number of American scholars, including John Wild,
James M. Edie, Bruce Wilshire, and Lester Embree.[3] Others have turned to
James for guidance in their positivist and linguistic analytic projects.[4]
In contrast with such interpretations is the continuing effort to under-
stand James as a prototypical process philosopher, an effort that was
perhaps initiated a half century ago by Victor Lowe.[5] Still others, like
John E. Smith, Charlene Haddock Seigfried, John J. McDermott, Ellen Kappy
Suckiel, and Daniel N. Robinson have selected particular themes in James's
Principles for amplification in metaphysics, philosophical psychology,
epistemology, and social philosophy.[6] For some a return to James promises
to dispell "the illusion of technique" that oppresses our culture; for
others the edifying moments that might curb the analytic malaise that
oppresses our philosophy.[7]

The publication of James's **Principles** marked a watershed in American
psychology, so much so that Jay Wharton Fay, **the** historian and apologist
for earlier American psychologies, has entitled his work, **American Psychology before William James.** In an address delivered in 1898 the psychologist J. M. Cattel asserted, "the history of psychology here prior to
1880 could be set forth as briefly as the alleged chapter on snakes in a
certain natural history of Iceland - 'There are no snakes in Iceland.'"[8]
While Cattell's remark should be put down as a mere witticism, as Fay's
study reveals, it is minimally true if the term "psychology" be restricted
to psychology as a natural (or experimental) science.

Following the lead of the German practitioners of experimental psychology, and with a background in medicine and physiology, James pioneered
scientific psychology in America. As early as 1875 he wrote his friend,
Thomas Ward, from Berlin: "It seems to me that the time has come for
psychology to be a science..."[9] In 1867 he offered a graduate course on
"The Relations between Physiology and Psychology," and in connection with
this course he and his students conducted experiments in a specified
place, **having** then, if not **founding,** the first psychological laboratory in
America.[10] Although James championed the experimental method in psycho-

logy, he often expressed his personal distaste for it, as when he face-
tiously remarked:

> This method taxes patience to the utmost, and could hardly have
> arisen in a country whose natives could be bored. Such Germans as
> Weber, Fechner, Vierordt, and Wundt obviously cannot.[11]

Nevertheless, James occasionally experimented in psychology, taught others
to do so, and consequently advanced the adoption of the method of experimentation in psychology. The Preface to the **Principles** may be read, indeed, as the charter for the establishment of psychology as a natural
(or experimental) science. As James wrote:

> I have kept close to the point of view of natural science
> throughout the book. . . This book assuming that thoughts and
> feelings exist and are vehicles of knowledge, thereupon contends that
> psychology when she has ascertained the empirical correlation of the
> various sorts of thought or feeling with definite conditions of the
> brain, can go no farther - can go no farther, that is, as a natural
> science. If she goes farther, she becomes metaphysical. . . . In this
> strictly positivistic point of view consists the only feature of it
> for which I feel tempted to claim originality. (P, I, p. 6)

Upon publication the **Principles** was greeted by an international, yet
mixed reception, thrusting its author into the front ranks of psychology,
where in reputation his sole rival was Wilhelm Wundt. Among his many
reviewers were the American philosophers, Charles Peirce and George
Santayana. In the **Nation** Peirce hailed it as "the most important contribution that has been made to the subject for many years"; and continuing in
his characteristically cranky fashion, he carped on James for indulging in
"idiosyncracies of diction and tricks of language such as usually spring
up in households of great talent." Further, Peirce charged James with
uncritical acceptance of data and failure to adhere to the rigorous logic
of scientific method.[12] In the **Atlantic**, George Santayana, whose own
philosophy, particularly in **The Sense of Beauty** and **The Life of Reason,**
borrowed heavily from James's psychology, greeted the **Principles** as a book
that is "rich and living, in which a generous nature breaks out at every
point, and the perennial problems of the human mind are discussed so

modestly, so solidly, with such a deep and pathetic sincerity." R. B. Perry has correctly called Santayana's review "admirably penetrating." For in graceful, inimitable prose Santayana perspicaciously grasped the essence of James's theory when he summed it up in a sentence: "the human mind is a series of single sensations, each of which has the whole brain for its cause and the whole world for its object."13

John Dewey discussed the Principles on many occasions, praising its role in converting him from absolutism to experimentalism and esteeming its centrality to the development of philosophy and psychology. On the occasion of the centenary of the birth of William James celebrated at the New School for Social Research in New York City, he designated it "the greatest among the great works of William James."14 Dewey's debt to James is inestimable, and he often admitted it, as when in the 1903 letter by which he transmitted a copy of the University of Chicago Decennial volume, Studies in Logical Theory, he wrote James: "...so far as I am concerned your Psychology is the spiritual progenitor of the whole industry. . . ." And in another letter written later during the same year he responded to James's suggestions:

> But when you say it [Studies in Logical Theory] needs psychological development I wonder sometimes if you fully appreciate how much all of this is in your two volumes of psychology. I have a good mind sometime to make an inventory of all the points in which your psychology 'already' furnishes the instrumentalities for a pragmatic logic, ethics, and metaphysics.15

Over half a century ago Dewey pointed out that there are two strains in James's Principles, one defined by the traditional method of introspection in psychology, the other by the experimental method.16 Of course he favored the experimental method, for it opened the way for the exploration of psychology and behavior, crucial to the development of psychology into a science. Yet each of these methods bore fruit in James's employment, affecting the subsequent courses of philosophies. It is beyond my compass here and now to touch on all the topics James explored by these methods - habit, instinct, emotion, to mention but a few, which I shall pass by; yet surely it is worthy of mention that often James's treatments were received appreciatively not only in academic halls but in the general culture outside.

Whereas the method of introspection, having served the advocates of the associationist psychology of traditional British empiricism for so long so well, yielded for James the doctrine of the stream of consciousness, with which he demolished associationism, it was the new experimental method that reached behind consciousness, uncovered the physiological basis of mind in the brain and other bodily activities of the muscles and nerves, and further illuminated the expression of mind in behavior. The experimental method ushered in psychology as a natural science, first functionalist, then behaviorist, and now, as if returning to James, functionalist again in the revival of the study of physiology for psychology and in the emergence of cognitive science.

The separation of psychology as a science from philosophy rests upon the assuptions which only metaphysics, not science, can explain and justify. In recognizing the difference between psychology as a science and metaphysics, James engaged in a kind of inquiry that is neither science nor metaphysics; it is what I have elsewhere called **philosophical psychology.** Philosophical psychology analyzes and defines the fundamental concepts of psychology. It examines the methods of psychology. It circumscribes the field of psychology, and lays bare its basic assumptions. It scrutinizes the intrusions of metaphysics into psychology and halting it from distorting the procedures or the results of science, it even expels metaphysics from psychology, as James sought to do in his critiques of the automaton theory with its doctrine of epiphenomenalism, of the mind-stuff theory, of the material-monad theory, and of the soul theory. In addition, philosophical psychology detects themes that stretch beyond the limits of psychology as a science and that invite metaphysical speculation and moral reflection. Let me suggest - and on this important point I am pleased to report the concurrence of Don S. Browning in his brilliant book, **Pluralism and Personality, William James and Some Contemporary Cultures of Psychology** - that today James's **Principles of Psychology** should be studied as a contribution to philosophical psychology, perhaps the greatest contribution ever made.[17]

The assumptions upon which James contended psychology as a natural science rests were explicitly formulated in the Preface to the **Principles.**

> Psychology, the science of finite individual minds, assumes as its data (1) **thoughts and feelings,** and (2) a physical world in time and space with which they coexist and which (3) **they know...** [P]sychology when she has ascertained the empirical correlation of the various sorts of thought and feeling with the definite conditions of the brain, can go no farther. . . . (P. I, p. 6)

So in the **Principles** James professed dualism in a twofold sense: the psychophysical dualism of mind (or consciousness) and body (or brain), and the epistemological dualism of thoughts and feelings in the mind correlated with external objects in the world.

It may be pertinent to recall that the golden age of American philosophy in which James was the preeminent figure was marked, as one of our leading historians has put it, by "the damnation of Descartes."[18] To James belongs credit for making the dualistic assumptions explicit, and ultimately for participating in the philosophical enterprise of overhauling and overcoming them. Elsewhere I have suggested that the presence of these dualistic assumptions in the **Principles** is evidence of just how entrenched dualism was at the beginning of the era in philosophy that A. O. Lovejoy dubbed "the revolt against dualism."[19] When James formulated dualism as assumptions that, in spite of being required by science in its present state, call ultimately for metaphysical justification, he exposed it to the philosophical critique and reconstruction that followed, and to which he himself contributed grandly in his works on pragmatism, radical empiricism, and pluralism.

James described the relations of mind and body, or of consciousness and brain, as "the ultimate of ultimate problems" (P. I, p. 178). In the **Principles** he posited a variety of empirical parallelism that correlates states of consciousness with physical events in the body. Further, he affirmed a form of causal interaction, so that consciousness can perform for the brain the role of a regulator harnessing an unstable machine in the service of ends. In the first chapter of the **Principles** James defined psychology and mind; in the second chapter he discussed the functions of the brain.

A doctor of medicine and a physiologist, James approached the philosophy of mind from biology. An adherent of the evolutionary biology of Charles Darwin, he applied the scientific theory of evolution to psychology. Here, indeed, is a major trait of the revolution in psychology and philosophy that he wrought. He defined mind or consciousness in terms of purposiveness, locating its mark or criterion in "the pursuance of future ends and the choice of means for their attainment" (P, I, p. 8). And he traced the development and function of mind in organisms. Thus he fathered functionalism in psychology although the term was invented and the movement arose later.

James began with the fundamental situation in which an organism interacts with its environment; he sketched the reflex arc, which was to win Dewey so much of his early fame. Further, James distinguished within an organism its mind (or consciousness) from its body (including especially the brain). Drawing upon the most advanced empirical research of his time to illuminate the foundation of mind (or consciousness) in the brain, he acknowledged the relevance of physiology for psychology and advanced a line of inquiry that, despite its interruption for several decades after his death, has recently been resumed.[20]

At the same time James retained mind (or consciousness), ascribing to it an essential function in the lives of organisms with highly developed cerebrums. Thus he viewed mind (or consciousness) as a kind of instrument that works in the interval between stimulus and response, particularly when action is blocked. Mind not only effectuates the adjustment of the organism to its environment but also guides the choice of means, altering the environment, in order that the organism may better attain its own ends. Consciousness is, in James's words, a **"fighter for ends"** (P, I, p. 144).

While working within a dualistic framework, then, James began the movement to overcome psychophysical dualism. In stressing the biological basis of mind, James initiated a revolution that was to continue in later American pragmatism and instrumentalism and that, when allied with social science, was to shape the thought of John Dewey and George Herbert Mead. For in the **Principles** James demonstrated that mind (or consciousness), instead of dwelling in a separate domain, is intimately connected with its natural environment. Interests rooted in biology and becoming conscious as ends direct all human mental processes and activities, influencing reasoning, knowing, and believing. While bridging the gulf between mind and body in a natural environment, James also broke down the traditional faculty psychology that had long segregated emotion, will, and cognition. He advanced the recognition, in Dewey's words, "that experience is an intimate union of emotion and knowledge."[21]

Application of the method of introspection in James's hands had borne the influential doctrine of the stream of consciousness, a doctrine with a decisive impact on our general culture. This doctrine, anticipated by the British philosopher, Shadworth Hodgson, whom James studied, admired, and cited, is presented in Chapter 9 of the **Principles**, reprinted in part from an article "On Some Omissions of Introspective Psychology," which originally appeared in **Mind** in January 1884. James portrayed consciousness as a stream: personal, always changing, sensibly continuous, dealing with objects other than itself, and choosing among them. By means of an appeal to direct experience, by introspection, James reported that he found consciousness to be a moving multiplicity of objects and relations from which so called sensations are produced by discriminative attention, and so he undermined the traditional empiricist concept of consciousness. In brief, for the picture of consciousness as a static mosaic he substituted the picture of consciousness as a stream.

In the picture of consciousness as a stream James found relations to be as immediate as the qualities they relate. As James said, "We ought to say a feeling of **and,** and a feeling of **if,** a feeling of **but,** and a feeling of **by,** quite as readily as we say a feeling of **blue** and a feeling of **cold**" (P, I, p. 238). So he anticipated a cardinal tenet of his later radical empiricism, although, as Professor Seigfried has demonstrated in the first chapter of her probing study of William James, **Chaos and Context,** the theory of relations in the **Principles** needed further reworking. In addition to the felt relations within the objective field of consciousness, James found felt connections between the transitive states of consciousness, upon which he rested the sense of personal self-identity. Further, in his discussion of how the images or data of consciousness relate to others not present, he introduced the terminology of "halo," "fringe," "horizon," "topic of thought," and "object of thought," which caught on in subsequent phenomenological analyses.

In the picture of consciousness as a stream, James also considered consciousness as dealing with objects; he therefore found intentionality to be a mark of consciousness. Intentionality in James is twofold: cognitive and volitional. In cognition consciousness refers to objects that exist independently of it. Moreover, the objects with which it deals depend, in part, on its own selection; they are the objects to which it attends, and attention is a volitional act.

Here in the juxtaposition of consciousness and its objects is the fundamental epistemological dualism of Subject and Object that psychology allegedly assumes. Toward epistemology James's attitude in the **Principles** was ambivalent, as he searched for a coherent theory of knowledge that embraces themes from empiricism and rationalism.[22] On the one hand, James dismissed **Erkenntnistheorie,** the critique of the faculty of knowledge as practiced by the post-Kantians, on the grounds that it is vacuous inquiry into the possibility of knowledge in general for the sake of establishing absolute foundations. On the other hand, he proposed the criticism of knowledge on the part of psychology. For assuming the existence of knowledge, psychology criticizes and explains "the knowledge of particular men about particular things that surround them" (P, I, p. 184). In effect, James prepared the way for the major revolution in Anglo-American philosophy in the 20th century; he transferred epistemology from metaphysics to scientific psychology, and within epistemology he brought into question and transcended foundationalism.

On the topic of epistemological foundations James vacillated. Often he intimated that knowledge rests on secure empirical foundations, as when he wrote: "Sensations are the stable rock, the **terminus a quo** and the **terminus ad quem** of thought" (P, II, p. 657). But on the whole, James passed beyond empirical foundationalism, because he held that sensations themselves are the products of discrimination in experience. Indeed, I would argue that James was a contextualist. Epistemologically, contextualism holds that knowledge is bound to the context in which it is achieved, so that what is basic to knowledge is context-dependent. As there is a shift in contexts, the basis of knowledge may be sensations or it may be conceptual meanings. Since, moreover, context is a matter of choice, it depends upon the selective interest of the knowing organism.

Throughout the **Principles,** therefore, the seeds of James's later pragmatism are strewn. Interests guide the cognitive activities of the conscious organism. Reasoning, general ideas, definition, classification are construed to be teleological; they are tools of the conscious, interested organism as it copes with its environment to further its ends. James was the first to name and discard the spectator theory of knowledge, and to portray knowledge as instrumental to the active organism. James, however, extended his theory to the way knowledge and action, cognition and emotion, fact and value, are fused, to the point that practicality is not for him the primary mark of reality. For he held that interest determines belief in reality and moulds the sense of reality. Chapter XXI of the **Principles,** entitled "Perception and Reality," is, with revisions and additions, the reprint of an article that James published in **Mind** in 1889 under the title of "The Psychology of Belief." Anticipating theories of the **Lebenswelt** espoused in later phenomenology and social psychology, James sketched seven belief systems, each correlated with a distinctive world invested with reality, from the universe revealed in common sense experience to the wildest constructions of madness. As James maintained:

> [R]eality means simply relation to our emotional and active life. . . . In this sense, whatever excites and stimulates our interest is real. (P, II, p. 924)

Yet in the concluding chapter of the **Principles** James espoused a complex theory of necessary truth. Long before W. V. Quine and Morton White, he denied the analytic-synthetic distinction (P, II, p. 1255 n). But he upheld a theory of the **a priori** and even argued that some **a priori** propositions are true. **A priori** propositions, he contended, arise not from experience but from the native structure of the human mind, and to some extent his theory foreshadows the conceptual pragmatism of C. I. Lewis. Always a physiologist, however, he grounded the **a priori** not in the social structures of communication - language - but in the human brain.

In the picture of consciousness as a stream James accentuated the characteristics of the personal. That every thought is a part of personal consciousness meant for James that a thought always belongs to an individual personal consciousness, and to that consciousness exclusively. "Absolute insulation, irreducible pluralism," he asserted, "is the law" (P, I p. 221). Add to this his argument against the theory of compound consciousness - namely, that any combination of units of consciousness is **known** only as effects upon some consciousness not included in the compound. The upshot was that later when in his radical empiricism James held that the same part of pure experience could be contained in more than one context, - say, a fire as imagined in a mind, and the same fire causally effective in a physical fireplace - he found himself in difficulty. Sensitive to this contradiction in his thought, James wrestled with it in his pluralistic metaphysics near the end of his life.

From the survey of personal consciousness James took up the issue of the consciousness of self. He steered a course midway between the empiri-

cist conception of the self as a bundle of perceptions and the spiritualist conception of the self as a substantial soul. He rejected both conceptions: the empiricist because it failed to do justice to the unity of
personal consciousness; and the spiritualist because it never could be
verified in experience. More pertinently, he transformed the issue from a
metaphysical question concerning the nature of the self into a psychological question concerning the sense of the self in consciousness, the
sense of personal identity, self-consciousness. His stress on the personal
was to feed into the mainstream of American personalistic idealism, particularly through the work of his student, Mary Whiton Calkins. His conception of the social self and his distinction between the "I" and the "me"
as functional aspects of personal consciousness were adopted and
transmuted in the social psychology of George Herbert Mead. His account of
the thinker as the passing thought, accompanied by an undeveloped theory
of appropriation, anticipated Whiteheadian doctrines of prehension, subjective form, and concrescence.

Consciousness, according to James, flows in pulses, each of which
appropriates past thoughts and is in turn appropriated by succeeding
thoughts so long as its personal form survives. Each pulse of consciousness is what he called "the passing thought." It is "a vehicle of choice
as well as cognition: among the choices it makes are these appropriations,
or repudiations of its 'own.' But the Thought never is an object in its
own hands, it never appropriates or disowns itself" (P, I, p. 323).
Feelings of warmth and intimacy accompany those mental states each of us
individually recognizes as his own, and these feelings cluster about one's
own body. The centrality of the body in the sense of the self, the import
of bodily feelings, seems extraordinarily contemporary, and startling in a
writer of the Victorian age. The appropriations of the thought, James
continued, "are therefore less to **itself** than to the most intimately felt
part of of its present Object, the body, and the central adjustments,
which accompany the act of thinking, in the head. **These are the real
nucleus of our personal identity**" (P, I, p. 323). And James concluded,
"The passing thought then seems to be the Thinker..."(P, I, 324)

Later in his 1904 article, "Does 'Consciousness' Exist?" James was to
raise a question in the title and offer an answer in the text which have
stimulated considerable commentary and controversy. In the aftermath John
Dewey and Milic Capek, to mention two, have participated on opposite

sides.[23] In either case, the intellectual provocation of James's treatment of the consciousness of self is undeniable.

In spite of James's disclaimer, metaphysics keeps bursting out of the pages of the **Principles,** whether it be in his treatment of time with the notion of the "specious present" or the theory of conception with the realist-nominalist controversy resolved or in numerous other passages. For James, however, the "pivotal question of metaphysics" is whether or not there is freedom (P, I, p. 424).

Central to James's psychology is volition or will. It is operative in attention and, further, in the effort of attention. Attention is the mental act of concentrating, intending one part of the flowing field of consciousness. What attention selects becomes an idea, and, on James's account, ideas lead directly to overt action unless inhibited by other ideas or obstucted by factors either in the body or in the external environment. Hence to attend, to have an idea is normally to act it out. The issue of human freedom then hinges on the question of whether the effort to attend is the effect of events transpiring in the brain according to mechanical laws or the expression of spontaneous, spiritual agency. Although science inclines toward the mechanistic hypothesis, James insisted that our feeling of reality, the sting and excitement of life, favored the theory of spiritual agency. However, he also insisted that psychology as a natural science could not resolve the issue.

In post-Kantian fashion James framed the question of determinism vs. freedom as a manifestation of the dualism of science and morality. Opposed to the scientific postulate that the universe is regulated by mechanical causal laws is the moral postulate that "what ought to be can be, and that bad acts cannot be fated, but that good ones must be possible in their place" (P, II, p. 1177). As for James's own position on the issue, he wrote in the **Principles:**

> Psycholology will be Psychology, and Science Science, as much as ever (as much and no more) in this world whether free-will be true of it or not. Science, however, must be constantly reminded that her purposes are not the only purposes, and that the order of uniform causation which she has use for, and is therefore right in postulating, may be enveloped in a wider order, on which she has no claims at all. (P, II, p. 1179)

What the wider order might be challenged James's speculative powers to the end of his life, and it provoked the philosophical energies of numerous American thinkers, especially John Dewey, who strove so valiantly to overcome the dualisms James so neatly defined. As for the lineaments of this wider order adumbrated in the **Principles,** the scholars disagree, some affirming naturalism, others idealism.[25] But in consideration of the influence of James on our general culture what has proved to be most original in the **Principles** and to have had the greatest and longest lasting impact on the public is not James's metaphysical speculations, nor even his hope for a scientific psychology. Rather it is his discovery and employment of the psychological point of view. From the psychological point of view questions concerning philosophy, morality, religion, and science are construed to be, not about objective topics as traditionally understood, but about the psychological processes of our feelings, attitudes, and beliefs toward these topics. The dominance of the psychological point of view in our popular, if not our academic, philosophy is in the contemporary American style, permissive, egalitarian, and affluent. It may well be the ultimate legacy of James's **Principles of Psychology** to American thought and culture.

Still we are philosophers, or at least students of philosophy, and James was one of us. In regard to philosophical enigmas, no matter how much they troubled him, he sought and offered no easy salving formulas. After all, in his day he had encountered quite a few such formulas - the Unknowable of Herbert Spencer and the higher synthesis of the Absolute idealists, to mention two he repudiated. What he said of them may reveal why to the end of his life he pondered the ultimate metaphysical problems - shifting back and forth, no doubt, but always within the early 20th century **Weltanschauung** of process and experience that he had helped to birth. Let me then conclude with a quotation from James. It may also serve as an exhortation to all young thinkers who, unlike James, would resort to formulas that excuse them from taking further thought.

It may be a constitutional infirmity, but I can take no comfort in such devices for making a luxury of intellectual defeat. They are but spiritual chloroform. Better live on the ragged edge, better gnaw the file forever! (P, I, p. 179)

NOTES

1. Robert B. McLeod, ed., **William James: Unifinished Business,** Washington, D.C.: American Psychological Association, Inc., 1969, p. iii.

2. Alfred North Whitehead, **Science in the Modern World,** New York: The Macmillan Company, 1946, p. 205.

3. See, for example, John Wild, **The Radical Empiricism of William James,** Garden City, N.Y.: Doubleday & Co., 1969; James M. Edie, "William James and Phenomenology," **Review of Metaphysics,** 23 (1970), 481-526; Bruce Wilshire, **William James and Phenomenology,** Bloomington: Indiana University Press, 1968, and Lester Embree, "William James and Some Problems of Idealism," **Der Idealismus und Seine Gegenwart, Festschrift für Werner Marx,** edd. Ute Guzzoni and Ludwig Siep, Hamburg: Felix Meiner Verlag, 1976, pp. 101-109. See also as the starting point of this line of interpretation in American scholarship, Alfred Schutz, "William James's Concept of the Stream of Consciousness Phenomenologically Interpreted," **Philosophy and Phenomenological Research** I (1941), 442-452, and Aron Gurwitsch, "On the Object of Thought" and "William James's Theory of the 'Transitive Parts' of the Stream of Consciousness," articles which appeared respectively in **Philosophy and Phenomenological Research,** VII (1947) and **ibid.,** III (1943), and which are collected in Aron Gurwitsch, **Studies in Phenomenology and Psychology,** Evanston, Ill.: Northwestern University Press, 1966, pp. 141-147 and 301-331. See also Andrew J. Reck, "Aron Gurwitsch's Place in American Philosophy," **Essays in Memory of Aron Gurwitsch,** ed. Lester Embree, Washington, D.C.: Center for Advanced Research in Phenomenology & University Press of America, 1984, pp. 261-265.

4. See, for example, A. J. Ayer, **The Origins of Pragmatism,** San Francisco: Freeman, Cooper, and Company, 1968. See also Matthew Fairbanks, "Wittgenstein and James," **New Scholasticism,** 40 (1966), 331-340; and William J. Gavin, "William James on Language," **International Philosophical Quarterly,** 16 (1976), 81-86.

5. Victor Lowe, "William James's Pluralistic Metaphysics of Experience," in H. M. Kallen, ed., **In Commemoration of William James 1842-1942,** New York: Columbia University Press, 1942, pp. 157-177. As a recent articu-

lation of the same sort of interpretation, see Craig R. Eisendrath, **The Unifying Moment; The Psychological Philosophy of William James and Alfred North Whitehead,** Cambridge: Harvard University Press, 1971.

6. John E. Smith, **Themes in American Philosophy,** New York: Harper and Row, 1970; Charlene Haddock Siegfried, **Chaos and Context, A Study of William James,** Athens: Ohio University Press, 1978, John J. McDermott, "The Promethean Self and Community in the Philosophy of William James," **Rice University Studies,** 66 (1980), pp. 87-101; Ellen Kappy Suckiel, **The Pragmatic Philosophy of William James,** Notre Dame: University of Notre Dame Press, 1982; and Daniel N. Robinson, **Toward a Science of Human Nature,** New York: Columbia University Press, 1982.

7. William Barrett, **The Illusion of Technique,** Garden City: Doubleday, 1978, and Richard Rorty, "Pragmatism, Relativism, and Irrationalism," **Proceedings and Addresses of the American Philosophical Association,** 53 (1980), pp. 719-738.

8. Quoted in Jay Wharton Fay, **American Psychology before William James,** New Brunswick, New Jersey: Rutgers University Press, 1939, p. v.

9. **The Letters of William James,** ed. by (his son) Henry James, Boston: Atlantic Monthly Press, I, p. 118.

10. Ralph Barton Perry, **The Thought and Character of William James,** Boston: Little, Brown, and Company, 1935, II, p. 22.

11. William James, **The Principles of Psychology,** Cambridge, Mass.: Harvard University Press, 1981, I, p. 192. Hereafter all references to this edition in **The Works of William James,** edited by Frederick Burkhardt, will be by means of the abbreviation P in parentheses incorporated within the text.

12. C. S. Peirce, **Nation,** LIII (1891), p. 15.

13. George Santayana, **Atlantic,** LXVII (1891), pp. 553, 555-6. Discussed and quoted in Perry, II, pp. 110-11.

14. John Dewey, "William James as Empiricist," in H. M. Kallen, p. 50.

15. Dewey's letters quoted in Perry, II, pp. 521, 525. See Andrew J. Reck, "The Influence of William James on John Dewey in Psychology," **Transactions of the Charles S. Peirce Society,** XX (1984), 87-117.

16. John Dewey, "From Absolutism to Experimentalism," in G. P. Adams and W. P. Montague, eds., **Contemporary American Philosophy,** New York: Macmillan, 1930, II, pp. 23-24.

17. Andrew J. Reck, "The Philosophical Psychology of William James," **Southern Journal of Philosophy,** 9 (1971), pp. 295-96. Don S. Browning, **Pluralism and Personality, William James and Some Contemporary Cultures of Psychology,** Lewisburg: Bucknell University Press, 1980, p. 49.

18. Max Fisch, "General Introduction," **Classic American Philosophers,** New York: Appleton-Century-Crofts, 1951, pp. 19 ff.

19. Andrew J. Reck, "Dualisms in William James's **Principles of Psychology,**" **Tulane Studies in Philosophy,** XXI (1972), pp. 23-38.

20. See David Krech, "Does Behavior Really Need a Brain?," in **William James: Unfinished Business,** pp. 1-11.

21. John Dewey, "William James as Empiricist," in H. M. Kallen, p. 57.

22. Andrew J. Reck, "Epistemology in William James's **Principles of Psychology,**" **Tulane Studies in Philosophy** XXII (1973), pp. 79-115.

23. John Dewey, "The Vanishing Subject in the Psychology of William James," **Journal of Philosophy,** XXXVII (1940), pp. 589-599; and Milic Capek, "The Re-Appearance of the Self in the Last Philosophy of William James," **Philosophical Review,** LXII (1953), pp. 526-644.

24. For naturalism, see Herbert Schneider, **A History of American Philosophy,** 2nd ed., New York: Columbia University Press, 1963, p. 498. For idealism, see Andrew J. Reck, "Idealist Metaphysics in William James's **Principles of Psychology, Idealistic Studies,** IX (1979), pp. 213-221.

ESSAY TWO

THE ANTHROPOLOGICAL FOUNDATIONS

OF

WILLIAM JAMES'S PHILOSOPHY

Michael H. DeArmey
The University of Southern Mississippi

Scientific psychology is always based on "an" anthropology, for it is not possible to investigate the particulars of human existence without some general concept of man as a whole.[1]

If our way of understanding the will could become general, do you know that it would be the greatest revolution in philosophy since Anaxagoras, Socrates, and Pyrrho.[2]

The philosophy of William James has received more than the usual share of rich and diversified interpretation. Indeed, James's admirers include language analysts, positivists, panpsychists, realists, behaviorists, and phenomenologists - virtually the entire range of movement in twentieth century philosophy. Each movement has attempted to appropriate James and scholars have enthusiastically claimed that James flew their banner. Focusing on **The Principles of Psychology** as a case in point, Andrew J. Reck writes that "James was first and foremost a scientific psychologist who had no use for transcendental psychology and its vagaries."[3] For Santayana, **The Principles** was most assuredly a "medical psychology,"[4]

The Philosophical Psychology of William James, edd. Michael H. DeArmey &
Stephen Skousgaard, Copyright 1986, The Center for Advanced Research in
Phenomenology, Inc. and co-published by arrangement with The University
Press of America, Inc., Washington, D.C., U.S.A.

17

while G. T. Ladd accused its author of an unfortunate "cerebralism."[5] On the other hand, H. G. Townsend, writing in 1934, described James's thought as a neo-transcendentalism with affinities with European phenomenology,[6] a view echoed by Bruce Wilshire, who writes that "if he [James] is any single thing, he is a pioneering phenomenologist."[7] James Edie, in the same vein, pointedly asserts that the doctrines of James and the phenomenologists are "intrinsically and necessarily fated to the same philosophical triumph or failure."[8] Donald Carey Williams humorously reminds us that James himself accused some of the greatest minds of his age of shamelessly misrepresenting his views, and suggests that James bewitched everyone by the sorcery of his phrases.[9]

While any new attempt to appraise James's philosophy risks being viewed as superfluous scholarship, I shall argue that a radical theory of human nature, a theory which has gone previously unnoticed, rests quietly at the foundation of James's thought. Careful study of James's writings reveals a basal anthropology which functions to unify several major strands running through his philosophical career. In the working out of this anthropology James's thought exhibits point by point the features characteristic of that group of thinkers on the continent of Europe who, beginning in the 1920s, spoke of their work as **philosophische Anthropologie.** Leading philosophers, such as Max Scheler, Helmuth Plessner, F.J.J.Buytendijk, Adolf Portmann, and Kurt Goldstein resembled James not only in their use of the phenomenological method, but also in possessing strong training and interests in biology and medicine. More significantly, their ambitions were to **unite** the important findings from both areas by means of a root conception of human nature. In order to demonstrate that James explicitly and deliberately attempted this unification, I shall first set out the features of philosophical anthropology in a way which will distinguish it from other disciplines. In the second section I call attention to some sorely neglected moments in the career of William James which go far in confirming the thesis that the proper framework for understanding James's thought is the anthropological one. In the final section I shall explore James's work in three areas representative of the reflective aims of philosophical anthropologists, topics in the philosophy of James which highlight his own radically **teleological** anthropology.

I. On Philosophical Anthropology

Philosophical anthropology is the third of three movements to develop on the continent of Europe in this century. The other two more widely known movements - phenomenology and existentialism - appear to have eclipsed the anthropological movement for a number of historical or extra-logical reasons. One American writer notes that philosophical anthropology "is virtually unknown in this country, although it has a good deal in common with what is called 'philosophy of mind.'"10

It is generally acknowledged that Max Scheler and Helmuth Plessner are the co-founders of philosophical anthropology, although this discipline can be traced back through figures such as James to Kant. Otto F. Bollnow accurately describes its beginning:

> . . . only recently has philosophical anthropology been developed. As an independent discipline it is a child of our century. Indeed, one can determine almost exactly the year of its birth. It is the year 1928. . .in Darmstadt at Grafen Keyserling's "School of Wisdom." There Scheler gave his worthy lecture under the title "The Place of Man in the Cosmos". . . thus, as a long awaited catchword had fallen, immediately. . . philosophical discussion was struck by his spell. . . But yet in the same year - 1928 - there appeared also Plessner's really extensive book, **The Stages of the Organism and of Man,** with the clearly expressed subtitle, "Introduction to Philosophical Anthropology". . . Scheler and Plessner can thus pass as the founders of philosophical anthropology.11

What is 'philosophical anthropology' for Scheler and Plessner? In one essay Scheler defines it as ". . . a basic science which investigates the **essence** and **essential** constitution of man, his relationship to the realms of nature (inorganic, plant and animal life). . ."12 Philosophical anthropology is not only then a fundamental philosophical discipline whose aim is the essential constitution of the human being, but is also an inquiry which does not forget (as phenomenology and existentialism do) that we are historical organisms, forms of life.

The contents of Scheler's lecture and Plessner's book reveal that both are informed by the biological/medical sciences and by the phenomenological movement.[13] Both Scheler and Plessner attempt to describe the eidetic features of human experience, and to correlate these with appropriate biological data pertaining to function and origin. But what genuinely unites both methods is the root idea of man, in the case of Scheler the idea of a person as a set of 'acts,' for Plessner the construal of man as the being with 'eccentric positionality.'

Continuing the survey, both thinkers consider it the task of philosophical anthropology to work out a theory of evolution illuminating human origins, to set forward a phenomenologically and biologically sound theory of the will (including resolution of the thorny problem of freedom of the will), to adequately portray the epistemic ties which bind man to man (including the problem of 'the Other'), to resolve the problems of mind/body and personal identity, and to reflect upon human destiny.[14] On the basis of this brief inspection, clearly philosophical anthropology is conceived as the fundamental philosophical discipline which will answer the large questions which we ask about ourselves. "Only such an anthropology," Scheler writes, "can furnish an ultimate philosophical basis, as well as definite, certain aims. . . to all sciences concerned with the object, 'man.'"[15]

Reflections on the writings of philosophical anthropologists, including James, lead one to specific desiderata for this discipline. First, it must be systematic; otherwise the 'topics' will be unrelated. An anthropology of excellence must be more than just another philosophical catalog on man. Secondly, phenomenological investigations should be viewed as confirming or falsifying theories of human nature. However, phenomenological essences and existential patterns must be 'situated' in the broader context of the physiological, historical organism. Exclusive attention to phenomenological or existential concerns opens the door to the charge of spiritualism, a criticism which James lodged against authors of "merely descriptive literature of the emotions."[16] Exclusive attention to biology leads to reductive and genetic fallacies, which James noted in criticizing "medical materialism" in the opening pages of his great study in human nature, **The Varieties of Religious Experience.** Thirdly, it should consider seriously the problem of a beginning. Where should an account of human nature begin? Is it merely a matter of style, or historical problematic? As we shall see, James begins, of necessity, with the problem of other minds. Fourthly, as mentioned above, this discipline must be comprehensive in the sense of asking and addressing the fundamental questions which we ask about ourselves. And finally, philosophical anthropology must be universal - applicable to all human beings regardless of culture-peculiarities. Indeed, it is desirable that this discipline state the conditions, in the nature of the human being, for the achievement of culture in general.

Additionally, philosophical anthropologists such as James, Scheler, Plessner, and others, who have more or less met these desiderata, all appear to concur in the view that their discipline is the logical successor subject to epistemology. All investigations take place in and through human nature, a conclusion reached in more restricted investigations by such thinkers as Rorty and Kuhn. Bollnow writes of figures in this movement as participants in a "profound killing of the foundation of the theory of knowledge in perception,"17 and Pappe notes that "Philosophical anthropologists set out from the conviction that the theory of knowledge has reached a desperate crisis."18 Different investigators have reached this position from different points of view: Erwin Straus from movement, especially upright posture; Adolph Portmann from the expression which we attribute to things and forms of life; and William James, whose pragmatism stems from the view of man as the being with 'open teleology.'

II. Anthropological Concerns in the Formation of James's Career

The decade or so from the early 1860's through the early 1870's is the formative one for the career of William James. Essentially, he had to select a career for himself from the areas of science, art, and philosophy. Above all he had to do something, for he appears to have lived under the childhood stigma that his father had no specific occupation. Simultaneously, the confluence of events on the European and American scene at this time were 'anthropological' in a profound sense. Never before or since has 'man' been the subject of such fundamental questioning, and James did not remain unaffected by it.

The fundamental questions about who or what a human being is came in waves during this period. First, the publication in 1859 of Darwin's **Origin of Species** called into question the relation of man to animal, and introduced a new impression of our deep past. As the author of the first textbook on animal psychology stated

> A question of the deepest importance to every system of philo-
> sophy has been raised by the study of biology, and it is the question
> whether the mind of man is essentially the same as the mind of lower
> animals, or, . . . is essentially distinct...Now seeing that upon
> this great and deeply interesting question opinions are now divided.
> . . It is evident that the question must be a large one.[19]

Darwinian evolution was hotly debated at Harvard, where James's beloved
professor, Louis Agassiz, was Darwin's chief American opponent, while
another of his teachers, Asa Gray, was a friend of the Victorian natural-
ist, and wrote the introduction to the first American edition of **Origin.**
The second wave involved the parameters of the human domain. During the
early '60s the Civil War was being fought, and during this horrible con-
flict questions pertaining to the nature and dignity of man were hotly
discussed. Two of James's brothers were for awhile amongst the "warm-
blooded champions of a better day for man."[20] Also at this time there
appeared the question of the equality of the sexes, discussed in works
such as Mill's **The Subjection of Women,** which James twice reviewed.

Yet another component in the maelstrom of basic questioning was the
new experimental penetration of the human being in the blossoming neuro-
sciences and psycho-physics. In 1867 James travelled to Germany to investigate first hand the new laboratory psychology being carried out by
Wundt, Fechner, Helmholtz, and others. At the same time neurology got off
the ground in the States as the result of the Civil War, which furnished a
rich field of patients with dysfunctions the result of injuries to the
head. James kept abreast of this work. One of his friends, Silas Weir
Michell, was one of the original founders of the American Neurological
Association in 1875, and another, the co-owner of James's mountain retreat
to whom a debt of gratitude is bestowed in the "Preface" of **The Principles,** was James Jackson Putnam, Harvard's first professor of neurology.
A new view of man was emerging from the blossoming neuro-sciences: all
behavioral disorders have their seat in the brain and are hereditarily
transmissible.

The effect of this anthropological maelstrom is not to be taken
lightly in respect to its impact on William James, a young man in his
twenties at the time, sensitive and intellectually ambitious. He became
suicidally depressed in the years 1867-9, and his letters occasionally
refer to the knife and the bottle. His escape from this 'crisis' was an

intellectual one, the working out of a new theory of human nature, which lifted him from being a morose young man in search of a career to a philosophical anthropologist of the first calibre.

James did indeed live in an 'Anthropological Age.' But that is not all. His early training shows his attraction to the dual methods (biological and phenomenological) employed by Scheler, Plessner, and others. First, his only degree was in medicine. He launched out from that basis as an instructor in comparative anatomy (from 1872-9), and wrote reviews of current literature in those areas (e.g., on Darwin, vivisection, circulation, lost limbs, etc.).

The other 'side' of James was the penchant for 'introspection,' which culminated in the phenomenological insights in **The Principles.** No doubt this interest was fostered by the transcendentalist atmosphere in his early home life. Townsend is probably correct in viewing his phenomenology as 'neo-transcendentalism,' i.e., transcendentalism made precise. At any rate, by the year 1875 James was presenting the case to President Eliot of Harvard for a new course at the graduate level, "The Relation between Physiology and Psychology". He argues for the course in a truely anthropological way, and for himself as instructor, on the grounds that he represents a "union" of both the biological and introspective approaches. His definitive plea for philosophical anthropology clearly transcends anything which goes by the name of psychology:

> The new course in psychology which I propose. . . the principle claim I shall make for it is its intrinsic importance at this present day, when on every side naturalists and physiologists are publishing extremely crude and pretentious psychological speculations under the name of "science"; and when professors whose education has been exclusively literary or philosophical, are too apt to show a real inaptitude for estimating the force and bearing of physiological arguments when used to define the nature of man. A real science of man is now being built up out of the theory of evolution and the facts of archaeology, the nervous system and the senses.
>
> . . . shall the College employ a man whose scientific training fits him fully to realize the force of all the natural history arguments, whilst his concomitant familiarity with writers of a more introspective kind preserves him from the certain crudities of rea-

soning which are extremely common in men of the laboratory pure and
simple?

. . . A union of the two "disciplines" in one man, seems then
the most natural thing in the world. . .[21]

III. Three Topics in the Teleological Anthropology of James

Earlier I mentioned the crisis period in the later 1860's. The seeds for
overcoming the crisis were already being sown in 1867 while James was in
Germany. Having become disillusioned with psycho-physics, he spent most of
his time reading Kant. One of the first books by Kant that James read was
Anthropology from a Pragmatic Point of View. He reacted to it with enthu-
siasm: It was a "marvelous, biting little work."[22] He also read the **Pro-
legomena,** Cousin's Kant, and the **Critique of Pure Reason** ("the honestest
piece of work I ever saw - there it stands like a great snag or mark to
which everything metaphysical or psychological must be referred"[23]).
Kant's thought, particularly in his **Anthropology,** is important in James's
development, for it formed the basis for a thoroughly teleological theory
of human nature.

The **Anthropology** contains a distinction between "physiological anthropology" and "pragmatic anthropology," which Kant describes as the
study of what Nature makes of man and the study of what man makes of
himself, respectively. Man is both Nature and Reason, and Reason is struc-
tured by what Kant calls "interests" (**interessen**), of which there are
three types - esthetic, moral, and logical. "Interests" is James's primary
term in his anthropology, where it functions as a canopy-word for diverse
teleological states (ends, desires, needs, wants, purposes, etc.).

In 1868, the year following the reading of the **Anthropology,** one
finds James brooding over what remains of the purpose of life, Darwinism
having banished any remnants of cosmic teleology. His answer is that human
teleology remains: ". . . the fact remains empirically certain. . . that
men suffer and enjoy. . . that enjoyment on the whole depends on what
individuals accomplish."[24] But what about science? How could he work out
the defense of human teleology against the medical materialists, and, back
home, against the 'nihilism' of Chauncy Wright? At some point between 1869
and 1872 James read Wordsworth. Ralph Barton Perry tells us that James's

favorite poem by Wordsworth was "The Excursion," in particular Book IV, with the interesting title, "Despondency Rejected." This portion of the poem contains a battery of arguments against determinism, in behalf of autonomy or self-determination, and nourished the seed of teleology planted by Kant. Scientists deaden the world by causal analysis ("Viewing all objects. . . in disconnection dead and spiritless. . ."25). But "there is laughter at their work in heaven,"26 because science has value only as a **guide** in the excursion of life, has value only in so far as it helps us "build up the being that we are."27 Some philosophers are just as lamentable as the reductive scientists, for even though the soul is composed of "twice ten thousand interests," they care no more for these interests than a mirror cares for the image that it reflects.28

Kant and Wordsworth then were two sources for the budding notion that man is the end-seeker. A third and last source is Charles Renouvier to whom I shall refer in the "C" subsection below.

We are now ready for the appearance of James's basal idea of human nature. While vacationing at Pomfret, Connecticut, in the summer of 1869 just after the completion of his medical degree, James sketched a view of man, his first definition of the human being:

(a) **Man** = a bundle of desires, more or less numerous. He lives, inasmuch as they are gratified, dies as they are refused.

(b) They exist by mere self-affirmation; and, appealing for legitimation to no principle back of them, are the lowest terms to which man can be reduced.

(c) Abridgement to extent of gratification (as in natural history, painting), and in degree (personal isolation, unfathomability of everything to our knowledge). The expansive, embracing tendency, the centripetal, defensive, forming two different modes of self-assertion; sympathy and self-sufficingness...

To 'accept the universe,' to protest against it, **voluntary** alternatives.29

This note, found in an envelope in James's desk shortly after his death, is both philosophical and autobiographical. It identifies human nature with a distinctive type of teleology - what might be called 'open teleology.' A being with 'open teleology' neither merely functions, as a machine or organ, nor does it merely possess goals, as do the animals, but rather can choose or 'affirm' goals. Ends or purposes in the human sphere can be weighed, arranged, discarded, created, proposed, etc. We human beings are esentially, irreducibly, and distinctively purposeful. The Pomfret note also calls attention to a dipolar structure inherent in open teleology. The human being can maintain his/her self by expansion, extending his being over a large 'surface' through a plurality of projects, or by contraction, restricting the scope or number of projects.

William James made a career of elaborating, refining, and defending the contents of the Pomfret note. Let us test the contention that James attempted a teleological anthropology of the sort I have described by focusing upon three topics, keeping in mind that we shall be looking for a root idea of human nature which is functioning to unify both phenomenological and biological investigation. I shall begin with the problem of 'other minds' because this is in fact the first problem James encountered in writing The Principles of Psychology.

A. The Problem of Other Minds

Scholars have neglected James's treatment of the other minds problem in The Principles because of the (misleading) impression conveyed in its opening pages. The reader is told that

> Psychology. . . asumes as its data (a) **thoughts and feelings,** and (2) a **physical world** in time and space with which they coexist and which (3) they **know**. . . the discussions of them [these data]. . . falls outside the province of this book.[30]

However, James finds that he must take up this problem in order to circumscribe the subject matter of his work. The psychologist, after all, does not study sticks and stones (except for their effects on minded beings). Strictly in line with the Pomfret note James offers this criterion, a teleological criterion, for mindedness: **The pursuance of future ends and the choice of means for their attainment are thus the mark and criterion of the presence of mentality in a phenomenon.**[31] James turns to phenomenological description and biology to explicate and defend this criterion. "We impute no mentality to sticks and stones," James writes, "because they never seem to move for the **sake** of anything, but always when pushed, and then indifferently. . ."32 Living things **appear** as self-moved. Moreover, their activity appears as tendential or obstacle-overcoming. Iron filings, blocked in their movement towards the magnet, remain blocked, but

> . . . Romeo and Juliet, if a wall be built between them, do not remain idiotically pressing their faces against its opposite sides. . . Romeo soon finds a circuitous way. . . With the filings the path is fixed; . . . With the lover it is the end which is fixed, the path may be modified indefinitely.33

In the later **Essays in Radical Empiricism** he amplifies this description somewhat, including the expressive features manifest in the appearance of a living thing, and the way activity of a living thing 'radiates' from a 'center' (e.g., the way limbs such as arms, legs, tenacles, etc., radiate from a central mass).34 James's strategy then appears to be this: He begins with the intuitively attractive connection between being alive and being minded, and undertakes a description of the essential ways in which a living thing appears in perception (he unpacks the extra-biological, or phenomenological, significance of "life"). He then is able to view the body of the other as both subjective and objective, in the way his own body manifests itself in his awareness.

Following the Romeo and Julliet passage cited above, James raises the question of whether conscious, goal-seeking behavior has been adequately marked off from merely functional, non-minded activity. To resolve it he brings in a physiological criterion: "The physiologist does not con- fidently assert conscious intelligence. . . until he has shown that the useful reslt which the nervous machinery brings forth. . . **remains the same when the machinery is altered.**"35 The physiologist then uses Mill's Method of Difference in conjunction with his perception of apparent telic patterns ("useful result") to infer mindedness. The logical structure of such inferences is somewhat more complicated in the attempt to locate the neural substrates for specific mental states, as James points out in Chapter II of **The Principles,** but the appeal to **telos** is still the crux of the inference.

Thus James's root idea of human nature begins with the appeal to both phenomenology and biology in the attempt to resolve the other minds pro- blem, the first problem in his teleological anthropology.

B.   Distinguishing the Human Being from the Animal

A second problem in James's anthropology is the differences between human beings and the animals. Part of the criterion for mindedness, as we have seen, is "choice of means" for the attainment of ends or purposes, and Chapter XXII addresses the topic of "Reasoning." Reasoning is a capacity or "means" possessed by human beings alone, James claims. It is the capacity for coping with unprecedented situations, for achieving our goals by circuitous routes.

In order to distinguish man from the animals, James selects Reasoning as the most obvious candidate. Focusing upon the syllogism, and using the writings of John Stuart Mill and W. S. Jevons, among others, he engages in what might be loosely termed a 'phenomenology of reasoning,' in order to ferret out the essential features or grounds of this capacity. He then seeks to ascertain whether these grounds can plausibly be regarded as essential to other **anthropina**: he cites wonder, self-consciousness, laughing, and language, along with reasoning, as distinctively human and similarly constituted. His account includes an appraisal of animal life as a test of the genuineness of the **anthropina**. I shall begin with that account, and then turn to reasoning.

Using the anecdotal method and analogical reasoning restricted by Lloyd Morgan's famous 'Canon,'[36] James concludes that animals are fitted to their environment like keys to locks. The parameters of an animal's life are fixed within a narrow framework of unalterable needs. The perceptual field of the animal is a hazy whole in which an object may stand out as a function of some need. Animals seem much like trance-subjects under hypnosis:

> . . . we have in this dispersion of the attention. . . something like a relapse into the state of mind of brutes. . . The trance-subject never gives any reason for his optical discriminations, save that 'it looks so.' So a man, on a road once traversed inattentively before, takes a certain turn for no reason except that he **feels** as if it must be right. He is guided by a sum of impressions, not one of which is emphatic or distinguished from the rest, not one of which is essential, not one of which is **conceived**, but all of which together drive him to a conclusion to which nothing but **that** sum-total leads.

Are not some of the wonderful discriminations of animals explicable in the same way? The cow finds her own stanchions in the long stable, the horse stops at the house he has once stopped at in the monotonous street, because no other stanchions, no other house, yield impartially all the impressions of the previous experience.[37]

The thinking of animals is at best by means of association by contiguity: A and B having been experienced together, the animal expects B upon seeing A.

1. Reasoning and Teleology. The chief feature of human reasoning is that it is not based on happenstance contiguity, but is rather housed in a project. Reasoning is always based on "a subjective interest,"[38] and "by dint of these [interests] alone," man is "sure to dissociate more characters"[39] or features.

Imagining the perceptual field stripped of interpretive elements, the object of perception would be a hazy whole in which some object stands out. The first step in the reasoning process takes place when the thinker "breaks it [the object] up and notices some one of its attributes."[40] Let S stand for the object, M for the attribute. Then, in relation to one's interest in S or M, one attributes some property to M. This is represented by the syllogism,

$$M \text{ is } P$$
$$S \text{ is } M$$
$$\text{--------}$$
$$S \text{ is } P$$

For example, if I were going to take my life and spotted vermillion on the shelf, I might reason that vermillion is a mercury compound, mercury compounds are poisonous, hence vermillion is poisonous. The controlling factor behind the syllogism is the purpose. Only for some purpose is an object indentified with some essence, or put into some class. What is important is not so much whether the object has that property, but what one wants to do in picking out that property. In connection with man, philosophers have no business in reducing man to a particle system; this is appropriate only for those researchers who are, for example, studying the electrolytes in the bloodstream. In thinking of things, James writes, we must keep in mind that there "are no truer ways of conceiving them. . . only more important ways, more frequently serviceable ways."[41]

2. Reasoning and Intentionality.   Intentionality is one of the grounds of reasoning. Following W. S. Jevons,[42] reasoning depends upon the substitution of terms, and such substitution requires "a fundamental psychic peculiarity. . . 'the mind can always intend, and know when it intends, to think of the Same.'"[43] Intentionality is not merely Brentano's 'directedness,' but the ability to identify and reidentify. Moreover, it takes place through a 'medium,' the regard or manner in which the object is intended. An object may be looked at in the aesthetic, moral, or instrumental regard, to mention just three. We appear to be able to switch or rotate regards. This third property of intentionality, implied by comments in Chapter XXII and more clearly presented in Chapter XXVIII in the discussion of thought-necessities, gives this feature of the mind a certain 'density.'

3. Reasoning and Imagination.   Also required in reasoning is the ability to hold together the S's, M's, and P's in the imagination. Reminiscent of Kant's first synthesis, James states that memory is not enough:

> We need something more; we need that the varying concomitants should in all their variety be brought into consciousness **at once**. . . uniting. . . and so permitting a perception of identical points.[44]

4. Reasoning and Intuition of Essences.   The ability to pick out a part (M) which lies embedded in the whole (S) James calls the "Perception of the Essence."[45] Aiming at the collection of items in the imagination, or fictively varying items, attention "shakes out"[45] an essence. This process, says James, is prior to conceptualization.[46] Spiegelberg, in contrasting James's empiricism with Husserl's **Wesenschau**, claims that James has "no room for any intuiting of universals."[47] Yet these essences, shaken from the fabric of the imagination, are neither particulars nor universals, but "floating adjectives."[48] to which either particularity or universality may be ascribed.

In his essay, "The Theory of the Three Facts," Max Scheler takes up the question of whether a pragmatist can have a place for phenomenological intuition in his epistemology. He appears to be referring to James. Scheler takes pragmatism as positing the organizing power of "practical needs" and states correctly that the pragmatist regards the senses as functions to "simply select out those sides and parts of the actually existent reality which can be made to serve as signs... which preserve the body."[49] Even with such an evolutionary account of the senses, says Scheler, the pragmatist can hold that

> The knowledge of the world which ensues on the occasion of this dialogue between the environment and the organism is not given through sense-functions but through an act of **pure intuition.** The performance of the act of intuition is merely triggered when the dialogue occurs and is placed in the service of life's goals.[50]

5. Other "Anthropina". These grounds of reasoning can be extended to accouunt for other features distinctive of the human being. The second **anthropinon** is wonder, a capacity which presupposes that we can reduce "the actual to fluidity by breaking it up in. . . imagination."[51] The third **anthropinon** suggested by James (without much commentary) is laughter, which requires "the recognition of identities in things different."[52] The fourth is language, "a capital distinction." The human child will begin to respond to signs if the sign is used "with varying concomitants." Soon the child will extract the essential feature of such signs - their use.[53] The final **anthropinon** is self-consciousness, which is possible through error. Error allows the child to dissociate his own act of thinking from what is thought of.

From this account we see that the features of reasoning support the idea of man as the being with 'open teleology,' as opposed to the closed teleology of the animals. Beyond the descriptive work of Chapter XXII are the correlative remarks about the biology of reasoning. An astonishingly large segment of our lives is everyday or routine. About such things as tying our shoes, or driving the car, we do not think. They are done by force of habit, "the enormous fly-wheel of society." Actions repeatedly performed soon sink below the level of consciousness, and their performance is carried out solely through the neural tracts, which simplify and make more accurate, thereby diminishing fatigue and freeing consciousness for other tasks. The 'wisdom of the body' is that it has the design of a teleological system. As we shall see in the final subsection below, the 'passing down' of what was previously a consciously intended action to a purely physiological activity is merely a miniature of the whole process of organic evolution.

Reasoning takes place in the cerebral hemispheres, a fact inferred from accident, disease, and surgery. These higher centers contain delicate and complicated webs of electrical activity. Some of this current apparently has inhibitory power, either preventing other areas from discharging efferent current, or allowing only internal or surface bodily change. Whatever physiological processes do occur ("the next task of the physiologist who ponders over the passage from brute to man"[54]), reasoning by analysis frees man from the otherwise practical import of the natural object. John Wild notes that for James man is the "hesitating animal," and that without that capacity we would be "conditioned by the unanalyzed object set before us."[55]

C. Evolution and the Theory of the Body

Ralph Barton Perry states that James's first problem in philosophy was the theory of evolution.[56] As a youth he adopted Spencer's theory, but this lasted only briefly, due to the criticisms of Peirce. According to the 'standard' interpretation of James, from that point forward he was a Darwinian, at least until his later years when he adopted Peirce's tychism. However, despite this longstanding tradition of Jamesian interpretation, there appear to be sufficient grounds for regarding him as a proponent of **selective, not** Darwinian, evolution. And the central feature of selective evolution is that it puts dynamic teleology back into the picture.

In 1868, when evolution theory was still sizzling in controversy, James discovered a little known French philosopher, Charles Renouvier, whom he thought "unequaled by anyone."[57] Renouvier was a voluntarist and pluralist, who saw nothing muddle-headed in an anthropocentric philosophy.

Encouraged by Renouvier, James began to transform Darwinianism vis-à-vis metaphysical pluralism, in a strategical defense of teleology. In 1868 reviews of Darwin, James claimed that the only 'law' at work in evolution was "Caprice," and that Darwin's theory was "only a descriptive or historical and not a physiological hypothesis."[58] A report from a student in "Philosophy 3" which James began teaching in 1879-80 described it as a course in which "Darwinism is to be treated metaphysically - precisely as Darwin and his followers say it should not be treated."[59] In an 1880 essay, James attributes the "triumphant originality of Darwin" to having "isolated" the causes which produce variation from the causes which pre-serve variation, regarding them as "different cycles. . . relatively inde-pendent of one another. . ."[60] James appears to accept Darwin's account of natural and sexual selection as partial explanations of preservation, but yet attacks Spencer's claim that the environmental feature to which the species becomes adapted produces the adaptation. During this very same period, in another essay, James rebukes Darwin for his seeming epiphenome-nal construal of purposiveness as something which ". . . floats off here and there accidentally as one of a thousand other physical results."[61] In order to "mitigate one of the strongest objections to the credibility of the Darwinian theory," James suggests that Darwinism be placed, in effect, in a broader teleological framework:

> . . . by its cognitive faculty [the animal] recognizes as well as Mr. Darwin which of its actions and functions subserves this good [survival]; would not the addition of causal efficacy to this con-sciousness enable it to furnish forth the means as well as fix the end - make it teleologically a fighter as well as a standard bearer?[62]

Interpreting James as a selective evolutionist enables one to readily explain certain puzzling passages in **The Principles,** as well as his peri-odic flirtations with Lamarckianism as late as 1887. Before I turn to those passages, I should like to explain in greater detail what is meant by "selective evolution."

Selective evolution, or as it is sometimes called, "the Baldwin Effect" or Organic Evolution, was first set out independently by James Mark Baldwin, Lloyd Morgan, and H. F. Osborn, in 1895-6. Baldwin explains the theory in the following way:

> Assuming the operation of natural selection. . . and assuming also that individual organisms. . . adjust. . . organisms which survive through individual modification will hand on to the next generation any 'accidential variations'. . . It will appear as if the modifications were directly inherited, whereas in reality they have acted as the fostering nurses of congenital variations.[63]

Sir Julian Huxley, an advocate of selective evolution, explains how the theory looks vis-a-vis genetics:

> Behavioral modification repeated for a number of generations may serve as the first step in evolutionary change, not by becoming impressed upon the germ plasm, but by holding the strain in an environment where mutations tending to the same direction will be selected and incorporated into the constitution. The process simulates Lamarckianism. . .[64]

Whereas teleology is the major feature of selective evolution, it is problematic on a purely Darwinian account. Selective evolution is supported by the evidence of exploratory behavior and imitation in animal groups, by the phenomenon of convergent adaptation, and by its explanatory power in explaining the transitions from, e.g., runners to flyers.

James's account of the brain shows the effects of adopting the view now called selective evolution. In **The Principles** he conceives of two types of brains: One would react infalliably to stimuli, but would be severely restricted in the number of stimuli to which it could react. The other could react to infinite variation and subtlety in the environment, but would suffer in its accuracy. If, however, a brain be organized around purposiveness, in the sense of conscious ends-in-view, then extensive variation and concomitant infallibility are possible. If telic consciousness regulates neural events by loading the dice "in favor of **those** of its performances which make for the most permanent interests of the brain's owner,"[65] then such variation and accuracy are possible.

James concedes that much biological discussion taking place at the purely physiological level involves such predicates as "interests," "survival value," "useful," "harmful," etc. This is the way we speak "when we are darwinizing."[66] Such predicates presupppose conscious ends or goals. For the organism survival is **pursued,** and behavioral demands are placed on the organs possessed by organisms:

> No longer is it, "if survival is to occur, then so and so brain and other organs work." I thas now become an imperative decree: "Survival shall occur, and therefore organs must so work!"[67]

What is true for bodily organs is also true for the brain. James accepts John H. Jackson's doctrine of levels in the central nervous system: in the course of evolution what was once consciously pursued passes down into automaticity, the brain as a whole being organized around "teleological modes of exercise."[68] In the literature only A. O. Lovejoy appears to recognize this aspect of James's anthropology.[69]

One consequence of selective evolution is that the anatomical/physiological features of each type of species are in part the product of the telic behavior of the members of its genealogy. The Cartesian bifurcation of man into disparate and contingently related realities is overcome. Leaders and heroes return from their 'primitive' and discredited lodgings to reassume importance.

D. Conclusions

It is far beyond the scope of this essay to attempt to identify and correlate the telic components in James's phenomenological psychology with his view of physiology just described (the whole chapter on the stream of thought is, for example, a thoroughgoing attempt, replete with 'tropical metaphors' from the Agassiz expedition to the Amazon, to describe the telic phases of thought, from the harmony or discord felt about the direction of our thought, to its incessantly selective character dramatically unfolded in the closing pages as 'carving out worlds.'). I have attempted to demonstrate that William James's phenomenological insights are part of a much larger program - the working out of a distinctive theory of human nature. I have tried to show that James is first and foremost a pioneering philosophical anthropologist, America's central representative of the anthropological movement.

The **Principles of Psychology** is the centerpiece of his achievement. Unquestionably a great book remained unborn when James's mentor, Chauncy Wright, died before he could answer the question put to him by Charles Darwin: "when in general anything can be properly said to be effected by the will of man."[70] It is one of those curious twists in the history of ideas that James's book should answer this question.

NOTES

1. P. Häberland, **Der Mensch** (Zurich: 1941), 91. Quoted in F.J.J.Buytendijk, **Woman: A Contemporary View.** Denis J. Barrett translator (Glen Rock, New Jersey: Newman Press, 1968), 23.

2. Letter from Charles Renouvier to William James. Cited in Ralph Barton Perry, **The Thought and Character of William James** (2 vols.; Boston and Toronto: Little, Brown and Company, 1936), I, 707. Hereafter abbreviated as "TC" followed by volume and page number.

3. "Epistemology in William James's Principles of Psychology," **Tulane Studies in Philosophy,** XXII (1973), 114.

4. George Santayana, **Persons and Places, The Background of My Life** (New York: Charles Scribner's Sons, 1944), 241.

5. "Psychology as a so-called 'Natural Science,'" **Philosophical Review,** I (1892).

6. **Philosophical Ideas in the United States** (New York: American Book Company, 1934).

7. **William James and Phenomenology: A Study of "The Principles of Psychology"** (Bloomington and London: Indiana University Press, 1968), 7.

8. "William James and Phenomenology," **Review of Metaphysics,** XXIII (1970), 486-7.

9. See Williams's essay in **In Commemoration of William James, 1842-1942** (New York: AMS Press, 1967).

10. Richard Schacht, "On 'Existentialism,' **Existenz**-philosophy, and Philosophical Anthropology," **American Philosophical Quarterly,** II (1974), 297. Marjorie Grene's appraisal is that philosophical anthropology was overshadowed by the appearance of Heidegger's **Being and Time**: See her **Approaches to a Philosophical Biology** (New York and London: Basic Books, 1965).

11. My translation of Bollnow's essay, "Philosophical Anthropology and its Methodological Principles," in **Philosophische Anthropologie heute,** Roman Rocek and Oskar Schatz editors (München: Verlag C. H. Beck, 1972), 19.

12. "Man and History," in **Philosophical Perspectives,** Oscar A. Haac translator (Boston: Beacon Press, 1958), 65.

13. On phenomenology as part of the anthropological programs of Scheler and Plessner, see Herbert Spiegelberg, **Phenomenology in Psychology** and **Psychiatry** (Evanston: Northwestern University Press, 1972), xxxvi and 16.

14. For a good English account of the work of five philosophical anthropologists, see Marjorie Grene's book cited in note 10.

15. Philosophical Perspectives, 65.

16. William James, **The Principles of Psychology** 3 vols.; Works Edition, Cambridge, Mass: Harvard University Press, 1981, II, 1064. Hereafter abbreviated "PP" followed by volume and page number.

17. "Philosophical Anthropology and its Methodological Principles," 20.

18. H. O. Pappe, "On Philosophical Anthropology," **Australasian Journal of Philosophy,** 39 (1961), 49.

19. George John Romanes, "Man and Brute," **Essays by George John Romanes,** C. Lloyd Morgan editor (New York: Longmans, 1897), 60-1.

20. William James, **Memories and Studies** (New York: Longmans, Green and Company, 1911), 41.

21. TC, II, 11.

22. TC, I, 512-3.

23. **The Letters of William James.** Henry James III editor. Two Volumes in one. (Boston: Little, Brown and Company, 1926), I, 138. Hereafter abbreviated "LWJ" followed by volume and page number.

24. LWJ, I, 130.

25. **The Poetical Works of William Wordsworth** (London: George Routledge and Sons, 1858), 292.

26. **Ibid.**

27. Ibid., 355.

28. Ibid., 350.

29. TC, I, 301.

30. PP, I, 6.

31. PP, I, 21.

32. PP, I, 21.

33. PP, I, 20.

34. **Essays in Radical Empiricism.** In **Essays in Radical Empiricism and A Pluralistic Universe,** Ralph Barton Perry editor (New York: E. P. Dutton and Company, 1971), 42 et passim.

35. PP, I, 20.

36. PP, II, 1005-5 and 979 note.

37. PP, II, 975 Note 0976.

38. PP, II, 964.

39. PP, II, 970.

40. PP, II, 957.

41. PP, II, 962.

42. See William James, "Review of W. S. Jevons's **The Principles of Science**," **Atlantic Monthly**, 35 (1875), 500-1.

43. PP, I, 434.

44. PP, II, 971.

45. PP, II, 968.

46. See PP, I, 478-80; 457-9.

47. Herbert Spiegelberg, **The Phenomenological Movement. A Historical Introduction.** 2nd edition. (2 vols.; The Hague: Martinus Nijhoff, 1976), I, 129 note.

48. PP, I, 447.

49. Max Scheler, **Selected Philosophical Essays**, D. R. Lachterman translator (Evanston: Northwestern University Press, 1973), 207.

50. Ibid., 208.

51. PP, II, 977.

52. PP, II, 979.

53. PP, II, 981.

54. PP, II, 989.

55. **The Radical Empiricism of William James** (Garden City, New York: Doubleday, Anchor, 1965), 196.

56. TC, I, 205-9.

57. LWJ, I, 286.

58. "Review of Charles Darwin's The Variation of Animals and Plants under Domestication," North American Review, 107 (1868), 367.

59. TC, I, 476.

60. William James, "Great Men, Great Thoughts, and the Environment," in The Will to Believe and Human Immortality (New York: Dover Publications, 1956), 221.

61. "Are We Automata?" Mind, 4 (1879), 7.

62. Ibid., 15.

63. James Mark Baldwin, Development and Evolution (New York: The Macmillan Company, 1902), 149-50.

64. Quoted by Sir Alister Hardy, The Living Stream (New York and Evanston: Harper and Row, 1965), from Huxley's Evolution, The Modern Synthesis, 2nd edition (London: Allen and Unwin, 1963).

65. PP, I, 143.

66. PP, I, 143.

67. PP, I, 144.

68. PP, I, 146 and 117.

69. Letter from Lovejoy to Philip P. Wiener, cited in Wiener's Evolution and the Founders of Pragmatism (Cambridge, Mass.: Harvard University Press, 1949), 265.

70. Quoted by Wiener, Evolution, pp. 31 and 253.

ESSAY   THREE

THE   PROJECT

OF

A   METAPHYSICS   OF   PSYCHOLOGY

IN

WILLIAM   JAMES'S

"PRINCIPLES   OF   PSYCHOLOGY"

Lester   Embree
Duquesne   University

I thought that by frankly putting psychology in the position of a natural science, eliminating certain metaphysical
questions from its scope altogether, and confining myself to
what could be immediately verified by everyone's own consciousness, a central mass of experience could be described which
everyone might accept as certain no matter what the differing
ulterior philosophic interpretations of it might be.

(Preface to the Italian translation, 1900.)

The Principles of Psychology by William James[1] is philosophically significant for, among other things, the project of a metaphysics of psychology
that one can find in it. However, this aspect of the Principles has
apparently been overlooked in Continental as well as Anglo-American
thought. While I might speculate historically on why this oversight has

The Philosophical Psychology of William James, edd. Michael H. DeArmey &
Stephen Skousgaard, Copyright 1986, The Center for Advanced Research in
Phenomenology, Inc. and co-published by arrangement with The University
Press of America, Inc., Washington, D.C., U.S.A.

41

occurred, I prefer to begin attempting to rectify it. Most of this essay is devoted to explicating James, but the whole is related to the following question. **Does what James offers about the assumptions of descriptive psychology merit the title of "metaphysics" as he comprehends** it? In other words, while I shall expound James's "discussion" of the data and assumptions of psychology as a natural science, the question beyond that will be whether his treatment is sufficiently "thorough-going" that he does not indict himself when he writes that "Metaphysics fragmentary, irresponsible, and half-awake, and unconscious that she is metaphysical, spoils two good things when she injects herself into a natural science" (I, 6).

Metaphysics and Psychology

The Preface of **The Principles** is chiefly devoted to contrasting metaphysics and psychology as a natural science. For James, both are parts of "philosophy" in the broad signification of "one Science of all things."[2] With respect to "metaphysics" in its own right, the fullest statement occurs in "The Sentiment of Rationality" (1879): "Metaphysics, the quest for the last clear elements of things, is but another name for thought which seeks thorough self-consistency; and so long as men must think at all, some will be found willing to forsake all else to follow that ideal."[3] Whether "metaphysics" in the Preface expresses a concept narrower than this will be considered presently. Where "psychology" is concerned, James specifically discusses mental life and while there is some psychotechnics in the chapters of **The Principles** on habit and attention, the account is otherwise refreshingly theoretical, i.e. not preoccupied with "application" in education, industry, or therapy.[4] Furthermore, since James discusses psychology in connection with physics, geology, chemistry, and physiology, it would seem "natural scientific" in something like today's usual signification. (As a student, James met Dilthey, but seems unfortunately never to have considered the possibility of a human-scientific psychology.)

With this preliminary comprehension of the general terms "philosophy," "metaphysics," and "psychology," we can look more closely at the relations between the latter two. Several passages, beginning with those in the Preface, express James's thought on this matter:

(1) "Every natural science assumes certain data uncritically, and declines to challenge the elements between which its 'laws' obtain and

from which its own deductions are carried on." We will return presently to the data of psychology. Two years after the The Principles was published, he illustrated this contention with another discipline.

> What is a natural science, to begin with? It is a mere fragment of truth broken out from the whole mass of it for the sake of practical effectiveness exclusively. **Divide et impera.** Every special science, in order to get at its own particulars at all, must make a number of convenient assumptions and decline to be responsible for questions which the human mind will continue to ask about them. Thus physics assumes a material world, but never tries to show how our experience of such a world is "possible." It assumes the inter-action of bodies, and the completion by them of continuous changes, without pretending to know how such results can be.[5]

(2) "Of course these data themselves are discussable; but the discussion of them (as of other elements) is called metaphysics and falls outside the province of this book." (But of course James had in the just previous paragraph of the Preface distinguished the "more 'metaphysical' chapters" from others and later omitted "all the metaphysical discussions" from **Psychology, The Briefer Course,** remarking on that occasion that **The Principles** "leaked metaphysics at every joint."[6] I construe this to signify that there is much metaphysics in the original book even though the intent was to exclude it.)

(3) Finally in the Preface of **The Principles,** and after seeming to contrast his own position with three other metaphysical positions, James writes:

> Of course this point of view is anything but ultimate. Men must keep on thinking; and the data assumed by psychology, just like those assumed by physics and other natural sciences, must some time be overhauled. The effort to overhaul them clearly and thoroughly is metaphysics; but metaphysics can only perform her task well when distinctly conscious of its great extent.

Different words are used in a seemingly parallel passage later in **The Principles:** "One must be impartially naif or impartially critical. If the latter, the reconstruction must be thorough-going or 'metaphysical'. . .

But Psychology is a mere natural science, accepting certain terms uncritically as her data, and stopping short of metaphysical reconstruction. Like physics, she must be naïve. . . ." (I, 141).

It appears, then, that while metaphysics in general is critically concerned with elements, ultimate clarity, and thorough consistency, there is also a specific metaphysics of natural science that is focused on the critical discussion, overhauling, and reconstruction of the assumptions that are naively undiscussed in the natural sciences, psychology included. What precisely "discussion," "overhauling," "reconstruction," and "critique" might signify and indeed whether they express coterminous, overlapping, or distinct significations remains uncertain, for James rarely uses and never defines them. Nevertheless, plainly he has a metaphysics/natural science opposition in view. The two endeavors relate in something of a traditional **first philosophy/second philosophy** fashion, but whether in the generalizing manner of Aristotle or with the subjective turn of Descartes and modern philosophy will need to be seen.

James's positive metaphysics might be sought through his opposition of it to three other metaphysical positions. First, there is the one in which a spiritual substance is posited behind the mental phenomena of an individual mind in order to explain them; he calls it "spiritualism," but we would say "faculty psychology." Second, there is the movement from Kant to Hegel and the British Hegelians in which there is posited an equally unobservable transcendental Ego that overcomes all oppositions. Finally, there is what we might prefer to call "atomism" or "associationism" but which James attacked as, among other things, "the mind-dust theory"; its elements are also unobservable, as are the unconscious processes of assembling them into phenomenal objects.[7] In opposing these varieties of metaphysics, James characterizes his own position as a "strictly positivistic point of view" (I, 6). If he had contended that the position that he calls positivistic were itself metaphysical (but from a passage quoted above we already know that it is "anything but ultimate") and if he had shown how it could perform the overhauling or reconstructive function with respect to the natural science he was most concerned with, then he would have offered a full-fledged metaphysics of psychology, one that was neither "fragmentarty, irresponsible, and half-awake," "unconscious that she was metaphysical," or "naif." Whether he did that or whether he indicted himself for spoiling both metaphysics and natural science is the question we can return to after considering what must be at least a "discussion" -

even if it is not a clear and thorough-going critical overhauling and reconstruction - of the assumptions of psychology as a natural science.

The Assumptions of Psychology

James's discussion of what natural-scientific psychologists should accept uncritically can be considered part of his "metaphysics of psychology," a phrase he did not actually use but which the now explicated thought calls for. The implicit as well as explicit thematics of this specifically metaphysical discussion consists of a number of interesting assumptions about the terms, relations, and methods of that science. We can return to the question of the standpoint of this discussion after reviewing them. In the Preface of **The Principles,** James seems to introduce three data, but actually there are two sorts of terms and two sorts of relations, for a total then of four items assumed. The terms are, on the one hand, thoughts and feelings (the concept of which shall hereafter be expressed with the more formal expression, **"the thought(s) studied"**) - James used "mental state" in the **Briefer Course** - and, on the other hand, **the physical world in time and space,** which I take to be an observable world since James the positivist accepts it. The relations are, on the one hand, the **coexistence** of the thoughts studied and brain states (brains being presumably part of the physical world) and, on the other hand, the way in which the thoughts studied know or **cognize** the physical world (and other things), "cognition" being a relation for James.

About the relation of **coexistence,** James writes: "I have . . . treated our passing thoughts as integers, and regarded the mere laws of their coexistence with brain-states as the ultimate laws for our science" (I, 6). He deserves praise for considering the brain the central organ where inbound neural impulses are integrated and for evading the constancy hypothesis over a score of years before Wolfgang Köhler denounced it and for instead wanting to consider the entire cerebral condition in correlation with the entire mental condition. Unfortunately, he actually offers rather little in detail about how the brain and mind condition one another, which is not to deny that he considers this issue metaphysical or believes the laws of such coexistence central for psychology as a natural science. Since his "metaphysics of psychology" is focused on the rest of his assumptions, i.e. the ones that cluster around the relation of cogni-

tion, further discussion about how James's general psychology is physiological seems unnecessary on this occasion.

If we confine ourselves to the assumptions that pertain to what can
be called James's specifically "descriptive" psychology, we have already
been told in the Preface that the psychologist assumes that **the thoughts
studied are cognitively related to the physical world.** Immediately we may
wonder whether the thoughts studied also cognize one another within and
between minds or streams of thought as well as how it is that they cognize, i.e. what "cognition" is, how the psychologist might correctly
investigate such matters, and, finally, how the relevant assumptions might
be accepted by James the metaphysician. Such questions lead us beyond the
Preface.

In the chapter on the methods and snares of psychology, James discussed four **"assumptions,"** a set which includes but transcends what is
told about the "data" in the Preface. Besides **the thought(s) studied** there
are **"the psychologist,"** "the thought's object" or, as he usually writes,
"the object of thought," and **"the psychologist's reality."** The following
illustration is offered, which interestingly implies that a psychologist
can somehow investigate the thoughts and feelings and the objects of
thought of subjects other than himself.

> To the psychologist. . . the minds he studies are **objects,** in a
> world of other objects. Even when he introspectively analyzes his own
> mind, and tells what he finds there, he talks about it in an objec-
> tive way. He says, for instance, that under certain circumstances the
> color gray appears to him green, and calls the appearance an illu-
> sion. This implies that he compares two objects, a real color seen
> under certain conditions, and a mental perception which he believes
> to represent it, and that he declares the relation between them to be
> of a certain kind. In making this critical judgment, the psychologist
> stands as much outside the perception which he criticizes as he does
> of the color. Both are his objects. And if this is true of him, how
> much truer it is when he treats of those of others! (I, 183)

(Since the word "introspection" has unfortunate connotations for many, let
me substitute the more neutral expression "reflective observation.")

In this example, the thought studied by the psychologist is a visual
perceiving that has its own object of thought, which is not the psycho-

logist's gray reality but rather something seen as green. The visual
thought studied, its green object, and his own gray reality together form
the psychologist's "total object" (I, 184). The relation between the
thought studied and its green object, as well as the relation between the
psychologist and his tripartite total object, are relations of "cognition." One might think that only an awareness (to substitute another
word temporarily for James's "cognition") that is somehow justified is a
cognition, but plainly the awareness of what can be denounced as illusion
is also "cognition" for James, who tends to use "knowledge" to express the
narrower signification definable as, perhaps, "justified cognition." Since
it is the basis for deciding whether the object of the thought studied is
veridical or illusory, i.e. known or not, the psychologist's reality is
the most important even if the least discussed assumption in Chapter 7.

In Chapter 21, however, we acquire some basis for construing what the
psychologist's reality might be. To begin with, it is clear from another
illustration that **the thought studied originally** believes **its green object
a** reality.

Suppose a new-born mind, entirely blank and waiting for experience to begin. Suppose that it begins in the form of a visual
impression (whether faint or vivid is immaterial) of a lighted candle
against a dark background, and nothing else, so that whilst this
image lasts it consitutes the entire universe known to the mind in
question. Suppose, moreover (to simplify the hypothesis), that the
candle is only imaginary, and that no 'original' of it is recognized
by us psychologists outside. Will this hallucinatory candle be believed in, will it have a real existence for the mind?

What possible sense (for that mind) would a suspicion have that
the candle was not real? What would doubt or disbelief of it imply?
When **we**, the onlooking psychologists, say the candle is unreal, we
mean something quite definite, viz., that there is a world known to
us which **is** real, and to which we preceive that the candle does not
belong; it belongs exclusively to that individual mind, has no **status**
anywhere else, etc. It exists, to be sure, in a fashion, for it forms
the content of that mind's hallucination; but the hallucination
itself, though unquestionably it is a sort of existing fact, has no
knowledge of **other** facts; and since those **other** facts are the realities **par excellence** for us, and the only things we believe in, the

candle is simply outside of our reality and belief altogether.

By the hypothesis, however, the **mind which sees the candle** can spin no such considerations as these about it, for of other facts, actual or possible, it has no inkling whatever. That candle is its all, its absolute. Its entire faculty of attention is absorbed by it. It **is**, it is **that**; it is **there**; no other possible candle, or quality of this candle, no other possible place, or possible object in the place, no alternative, in short, suggests itself as even conceivable; so how can the mind help believing the candle real? (III, 917)

If this is so for the thought studied with respect to its own object, the same would seem to be the case for the thought by which the psychologist investigates the thought studied and its object. What justifies, however, the privilege of the psychologist's reality over the thought studied's reality?

Further along in the same chapter, which is on the "perception of reality" (it was originally called "The Psychology of Belief"), James discusses what he calls "sub-universes." Among such sub-universes there is one called "the world of sense" to which, plainly, gray and green realities and candles against dark backgrounds would belong. If this were exclusively the psychologist's sub-universe in contrast to some sort of pre-scientific, everyday sub-universe, then we might begin to justify the psychologist's acceptance of the gray reality over the green appearance cognized by the thought studied through a relation of sub-universes, but James does not say that, even though the above quotation does refer a given object to a context of others. Yet the problem that has now been explicated, i.e. why is the psychologist's reality the real reality over against the object of thought that the thought studied always takes as real? certainly belongs to a "metaphysics of psychology."

It can be remarked at this point that there is mention by James of a role that seems higher than either the thought studied and its object or the psychologist who reflectively observes them along with his reality:

The complete philosopher is he who seeks not only to assign to every given object of his thought its right place in one or the other of these sub-worlds, but he also seeks to determine the relation of each sub-world to the others in the total world which is. (III, 921)

Presumably such a "complete philosopher" is a metaphysician as well as a scientist. Moreover, such a complete philosopher would have the "total world which **is**" as his object and that must include the psychologist and his reality, the thoughts he studies, and their objects. Finally, such a complete philosopher should be able to decide finally whether the gray or the green object is the real reality and thus be able to guarantee the authority of the psychologist over the thought she studies. Whether James has places not only for the psychologist and his reflective observation but also for the complete philosopher and her philosophical activities, at least where psychology as a natural science is concerned, is another way of putting the question to which the present essay is devoted, for certainly a metaphysics of psychology without such matters dealt with is fragmentary and unconscious of its full task, if not also irresponsible and half-awake.

If James's analysis of the four cognitively related assumptions of descriptive psychology (the complete philosopher would be outside that situation) seems narrow, let me quote another passage which includes action and context and shows how James is prepared to accept results of "psychical research." In this case, the thought studied is the dreaming of somebody's death and the psychologist's reality is that person's death.

> If the dream were the only one of its kind the subject ever had it its life, if the context of the death in the dream differed in many particulars from the real death's context, and if the dream led to no action about the death, unquestionably we should call it a strange coincidence and naught besides. But if the death in the dream had a long context, agreeing point for point with every other feature that attended the real death; if the subject were constantly having such dreams, all equally perfect, and if on awakening he had a habit of acting immediately as if they were true and so getting 'the start' on his more tardily informed neighbors, - we should probably all have to admit that he had some mysterious kind of clairvoyant power, that his dreams in an inscrutable way knew just those realities in which they figured, and that the word 'coincidence' failed to touch the root of the matter. And whatever doubts any one preserved would completely vanish if it should appear that from the midst of his dream he had the power of **interfering** with the course of the reality, and making the events in it turn this way or that, according as he

dreamed they should. Then at least it would be certain that he and
the psychologist were dealing with the **same.** It is by such tests as
these that we are convinced that the waking minds of our fellows and
our own minds know the same external world. (I, 213)

James of course goes much further in his efforts at reflective observation within the framework established by the four discussed assumptions
and produces his famous doctrines of the stream of thought, the specious
present, the topic and fringes of the object of thought, etc. But for the
sake of comprehending what is most immediately of concern for a metaphysics of psychology, we should now consider how the psychologist, for
James, ought and ought not to proceed in his research, i.e. his methodology in the strict signification.

James recognizes three properly psychological methods (I, 185-93);
explanation in terms of neurophysiological factors is another matter. He
believes no general description of the **experimental** method would be in-
structive to the uninitiated and hence merely lists some fields of its
recent application. The **comparative** method, by which one studies the
thoughts and objects of thought of "bees and ants. . . savages, infants,
madmen, idiots, the deaf and blind, criminals, and eccentrics" (I, 193)
(and in that day also probably the lower classes and women!), is supplementary to experimentation and especially to the fundamental psychological
method of introspection or **reflective observation.** What is observed and
thus known about in psychological observation is, as we have seen, the
psychologist's tripartite "total object." While reflection - according to
James - was infaliable for Franz Brentano and impossible for Auguste
Comte, John Stuart Mill is praised for advocating that one's own stream of
thought be analyzed in a retrospective as well as inwardly reflecting
manner, in order to get the "knowledge about" the thoughts studied and
what they cognize that psychology needs, and not merely the "acquaintance
with" them that even the baby in her crib possesses. Such descriptive
results are as reliable and corrigible as any other observation-based
knowledge:

Something is before us; we do our best to tell what it is, but
in spite of our good will we may go astray, and give a description
more applicable to some other sort of thing. The only safeguard is in
the final **consensus** of our further knowledge about the thing in

question, later views correcting earlier ones, until at last the harmony of a consistent system is reached. Such a system, gradually worked out, is the best guarantee the psychologist can give for the soundness of any particular psychologic observation which he may report. Such a system we ourselves must strive, as far as may be, to attain. (I, 191)

(And it might be that such a system and its metaphysically warranted ultimate consistency is the psychologist's reality as a sub-universe within the total world which is.)

Besides the recommendation of reflective observation as the fundamental method, James's methodology includes discussion of two sources of error. First, because it can lead us to believe that the thoughts studied are like things and also to believe in named unobservables, speech should be distrusted. Second, there is the psychologist's fallacy, which comes in two versions. One consists in mistaking what one as psychologist cognizes of an object for what the thought one studies cognizes of the same object and the other is a reflective version whereby what the psychologist cognizes of the thought studied is mistaken for what, if anything, the thought studied cognizes of itself. It is difficult to doubt that the discussion of these methodological prescriptions belongs with the discussion of the assumptions of descriptive psychology and hence pertains to James's "metaphysics of psychology."

Charge and Verdict

The question remains whether the "discussion" of psychology's assumptions in **The Principles** is sufficiently "thorough-going" to be considered an "overhauling" or a "reconstruction." Insofar as overhauling or reconstructing involves the challenging of previous metaphysical groundings (if this term be permitted), something of that can be found where spiritualism, transcendental idealism, and the mind-dust theory are concerned. We also know that metaphysical overhauling requires awareness of the great extent of the task involved. It is probable that James had that awareness. But is his effort sufficiently thoroughgoing, not necessarily for general metaphysical purposes, but merely for the purposes specific to a metaphysics of psychology? Although James does not say it, this would certainly involve at least a relating of the discussed assumptions to some general metaphysical position that he accepted.[8] It further seems probable that not to so relate them would make a metaphysics of psychology "fragmentary, irresponsible, and half-awake," if not also "unconscious that she is metaphysical." We have seen enough about the need for and the role of metaphysics to doubt that it was totally unconscious in James. Still, we need to know more about his own and positive position, i.e. his "strictly positivistic point of view," the only feature of **The Principles** for which - remarkably - he felt "tempted to claim originality."

James's positivism can be said to involve a rejection of metaphysical unobservables for the sake of description based on reflective observation. But beyond that, effectively nothing positive is said about positivism in **The Principles**! But it may be that "positivism" is a scientific as well as a philosophical approach for James and in relation to such a distinction we should consider some related documentation. In a letter to Marillier, a critic who subscribed to associationism, James wrote:

> The passing thought, which I propose that psychologists should adopt as their ultimate datum on the mental side, is expressly intended to make psychology more positivistic and free from subtle disputes than she has been. Practically all schools agree with common sense that we do have thoughts which pass, although they differ as to the genesis and constitution of such thoughts. Now I contend that all the facts of our experience are **formulable** in terms of these undecomposed thoughts, on the one hand, and of the 'objects' which they 'know' on the other hand, quite as simply and more naturally than by the (associationistic) theory of ideas. Formulating them thus gives us a good honest empirical body of science, which does not of course go to the bottom of all mysteries, but which, as far as it does go, is sound, and as free as possible from containing paradoxes and stumbling-blocks in its terms. The further questions which remain (as to the genesis and constitution of these thoughts, etc.) seem to me so subtle that they had best be relegated to 'metaphysics'; and it is the misfortune of the age in which I write quite as much as my own personal fault, that in trying to show how to make a psychology which shall be 'positivistic' I have had to exert myself also to show the metaphysical difficulties that the current theories involve, and of which they supporters seem so profoundly unconscious.[9]

James would seem to advocate more a scientific than a metaphysical positivism. Moreover, the objections to unconscious metaphysics are directed at others. Even so, where is the fully awake, responsible, and complete metaphysics that is called for? James gives little more than what has been explicated above. In the Preface to the Italian translation of 1900, he does remark: "I must confess that during the years that have intervened since the book's publication I have realized more and more the difficulty of treating psychology without introducing some positive philosophic doctrine" (I, 1,484).

In sum, unless the charges are dropped because the metaphysics of psychology that he did include in The Principles is "conscious" and neither metaphysics nor psychology as a natural science seem "spoiled," James is guilty, whether he knows it or not, of the charge he levelled against others.

What might have been done

While James did not adequately fulfill his own project of a metaphysics of psychology in The Principles, we can be grateful to him for showing the task. In gratitude, I might even attempt a sketch of how the task might have been performed in a manner James might have accepted as philosophically positivistic, i.e. founded on reflective observation. It is convenient to speak of levels in this connection.

On the first level, that illustrated by the baby and her candle, the thought studied cognizes its object, which it accepts as real. On the second level, the role of the psychologist is performed (perhaps on his own mind, perhaps on that of an other) and the first-level thought, its object of thought, and the psychologist's reality are all cognized. On the basis of the psychologist's reality, the first-level object of thought is judged veridical or illusory. This much is stated or implied in the early James.

But, as intimated earlier, one can ask about the point of view (or the level) from which the second level might be cognized. It would seem that reflective observation is possible on the second level such that a descriptive psychology of descriptive psychology be produced, but that could hardly perform the task of a metaphysics of psychology since it would remain a natural science with undiscussed assumptions and metaphysics requires discussion of assumptions and much more. It thus seems plausible to introduce a third level for James's "complete philosopher," whose task is more than that of psychology, whose field is "the total world which **is**," and whose aim is "a science of all things." From that level the assumptions, data, methods, etc. of psychology as well as any other natural science are no longer naively accepted but instead questioned, discussed, and even justified.

On such a third level, which could also be called "metaphysical" in something like James's signification, one could (a) rely on one's own ability to establish various distinctions and methodological prescriptions through reflective observation of second- and first-level thoughts studied, objects of thought, and realities, (b) have one's observations corrigible through further reflective observation by other metaphysicians, and (c) even reflectively establish the third level itself without recourse to a fourth level, there being in principle no naive assumptions left requiring consideration from such an additional level.

Had James proceeded in this way, he might well have developed a transcendental-phenomenological first philosophy before Husserl (but in the spirit of Descartes) in which psychology and other species of natural or, more generally, "mundane" science would find their critical grounding. While he did not, he did expose the task of discussing, overhauling, and reconstructing the principles of psychology in the book of that title and that is plainly something of philosophical significance.

NOTES

1. James, **The Principles of Psychology**, 3 vols., Works Edition, Cambridge, Mass.: Harvard University Press, 1981, I, 1. Further references to this source will be cited parenthetically within the text.

2. James, **Psychology**, The Briefer Course, New York: Henry Holt and Co., 1892, p. 1.

3. James, **Collected Essays and Reviews**, New York: Russell & Russell, 1969, p. 124. Cf. **The Principles**, I, 1,148 and **Psychology**, p. 461.

4. For James's **ultimate** purposes in psychology, consider this passage: "All natural sciences aim at practical prediction and control, and in none of them is this more the case than in psychology to-day. We live surrounded in an enormous body of persons who are most definitely interested in the control of states of mind, and incessantly craving for a sort of psychological science which will teach them **how to act**. What every educator, every jail-warden, every doctor, every clergy-man, every asylum-superintendent, asks of psychology is practical rules." **Collected Essays and Reviews**, p. 319.

5. pp. iii and 467.

6. **Essays and Reviews**, pp. 317 f., cf. 321.

7. Cf. Lester Embree, "William James and Some Problems of Idealism," in **Der Idealismus und Seine Gegenwart**, Festschrift für Werner Marx, edd. Ute Guzzoni, Bernard Rang, and Ludwig Siep, Hamburg: Felix Meiner Verlag, 1976. Besides James's critique of the three other metaphysical positions, this essay discusses the problem of the constitution of identity in the early James.

8. Ralph Barton Perry of course knew James personally and, while he does not claim it, may have had some authorized insight into this matter. His contention is that James already had his monistic metaphysics, Radical Empiricism, in reserve when he wrote **The Principles**, which then contains an incomplete epistemology and offers the dualism of the thought studied

and the object of thought as a "provisional doctrine." "In other words, his dualism was not a completely thought-out set of presuppositions for psychology, but a half-thought-out compromise designed to give him a temporary respite from philosophizing." (**The Thought and Character of William James,** 2 vols., Boston: Little Brown and Co., 1935, II, 72-75.) Such an interpretation supports the present questioning of the thorough-goingness of James's metaphysics of psychology.

9. Ibid., II 102. Cf. **The Principles,** I, 185 and the epigram at the head of the present study.

ESSAY   FOUR

ON   THE   METAPHYSICAL   FOUNDATIONS

OF

SCIENTIFIC   PSYCHOLOGY

Charlene Haddock Seigfried
Purdue University

Andrew Reck correctly notes William James's intentions in **The Principles of Psychology** "to stick to practical psychology and ignore metaphysical difficulties."[1] Despite this intention, it is obvious that James could not or would not eliminate metaphysical considerations from his psychological masterpiece. Rather than assuming, as Reck does, that James meant to assert the essential incompatibility of psychology and metaphysics, I am arguing that he deliberately set out to reconcile them, but only after carefully distinguishing the parameters of each by reinterpreting them. The intrusive metaphysical passages attest to a larger project of which the **Principles** is only the first step. This larger project involved founding psychology as a strictly phenomenal science, indifferent to either empirical or idealist philosophical presuppositions, in order to provide an experimental basis for developing a non-speculative philosophy. James could not altogether prevent his goal of a psychologically based philosophy from intruding on the immediate project of developing an appropriately neutral psychology, however, particularly since the precise relationship between the philosophic drive for ultimate explanations and the scientific drive for fidelity to immediate facts was yet to be worked out.

The **Philosophical Psychology of William James,** edd. Michael H. DeArmey & Stephen Skousgaard, Copyright 1986, The Center for Advanced Research in Phenomenology, Inc. and co-published by arrangement with The University Press of America, Inc., Washington, D.C., U.S.A.

In this early period James is not easy to place philosophically. At the time, for instance, he sympathized both with Berkeleian idealism and scientific positivism, although he rejected tenets of both positions. Likewise painfully aware of the incompatibility of German idealism and British empiricism, he was nonetheless committed to fundamental propositions of each. A lesser man, in the interest of consistency, would have chosen among these alternatives, but James was equally convinced of the importance to life of a systematic philosophical world view, epitomized by idealist philosophies, of the necessity for adherance to individual experience characteristic of Scottish common-sense philosophy and of British empiricism, and of his duty as a man of science to respect the increasingly atomistic and quantitative world scientists were assuming. He can be numbered among those troubled nineteenth century thinkers "who feel in their bones that man's religious interests must be able to swallow and digest and grow fat upon all the facts and theories of modern science, but who yet have not the capacity to see with their own eyes how it may be done."[2]

In the **Principles** James explicitly adopts "**the psychological** point of view, the relatively uncritical non-idealistic point of view of all natural science, beyond which this book cannot go."[3] And yet, as early reviewers already pointed out, philosophical speculation keeps intruding. Even in the abridgment, **Psychology: Briefer Course,** which he shortened precisely by eliminating all matters extraneous to a strictly scientific point of view, philosophical considerations are not absent. He declares in the last chapter, for instance, that "we can thus ignore the free-will question in psychology" and "can hand the free-will controversy over to metaphysics" because science can only deal with general laws of volition and not with independent variables. By definition "science is a system of fixed relations" and cannot judge, e.g., whether more or less effort may or may not have been called on in any case, that is, whether the effort actually used was determined by the whole set of previous conditions or not.[4] Following Kant, he held that such generalized laws of nature could neither disclose not contradict individual autonomy. Nonetheless, this conscious avowal of the absolute dichotomy between science and metaphysics occurs at the end of a chapter on the will in which, half way through, he gives as the motivation for carefully examining the conditions under which the feeling of volition and effort arises, the fact that momentous spiritual conclusions follow, particularly that of free will versus determinism (PBC, 431). He even ends the chapter with a section on the "ethical importance of the phenomenon of effort" (PBC, 454-6). Furthermore, his own interest in the outcome of the debate unabashedly colors his presentation throughout.

The most persuasive explanation of this seemingly contradictory behavior of asserting allegience to a positivist model of science while practicing an evolutionary, philosophical psychology is that James was founding psychology on a new basis and had not yet worked out all the implications of such a radical project. James recognized the unsatisfactoriness of dichotomizing science and metaphysics but programmatically adhered to this division in a sustained attempt to undermine the anti-metaphysical bias of positivist science. He did this by denying any constraints on it derived from metaphysical speculation while retaining its adherence to the experimental method. Even though he rejected the Comtean anti-metaphysical bias, he heartily embraced the empirical bias of positivism with its emphasis on experimentation. This dual project - of detaching the success of experimental psychology from its anti-metaphysical bias by neutralizing it, as it were, i.e., by limiting it to experimentally based laws and regularities unfounded by any metaphysics, and of using these purely factual, experimentally derived results as a fitting basis to construct a new and better metaphysics - led him both to uphold the science-metaphysics split to accomplish the first goal and transgress that split when necessary to point out the benefits to be gained in pursuing the second goal.

Rather than mere ambivalence, this dual goal accounts for what otherwise would be seen as occasional lapses against his own stated framework of a strict separation. This Kantian limitation of the scope of psychology precisely in order to make room for freedom is again illustrated in **The Briefer Course.** He says, for instance, that the refusal of psychology as a strict science to take up the issue of free will - the refusal to enter into a philosophical debate - ostensively because its self-definition includes protocols of verification which are inappropriate to it, actually constitutes a denial of the legitimacy of such inquiries. He reasons that psychology deals with human consciousness, and if free will never appears among the other phenomena being investigated, then it would seem reasonable to conclude that free will does not exist at all (PBC, 453). This conclusion, of course, is totally unacceptable to James.

Lest there be any doubt as to his intentions, the larger project appears in print a few years after the **Principles.** In "A Plea for Psychology as a 'Natural Science'" (1892), James most clearly sets out his view of the relation of philosophy and science to the newly emerging discipline of psychology.[5] He consciously presides over the birth of psychology as a science, out of "a mass of phenomenal description, gossip, and myth," clarifying the polemical intent of his recently published **Principles:** "I wished, by treating Psychology **like** a natural science, to help her to become one" (CER, 316-7). The article is a straightforward plead for a strict separation of a scientific psychology from a philosophical psychology, with scientists foreswearing philosophical pronouncements and philosophers refraining from imposing their standards on scientific psychology. But by keeping in mind the audience for which the article was intended and James's characterization of science and philosophy, a less straightforwardly separatist interpretation is rendered both plausible and preferable. As if in corroboration, James himself retracts such a sharp separation a few years later (address 1894, printed 1895) when he reluctantly admits that such a strict dichotomy is impossible in practice.[6] I will be arguing that James's immediate goal is indeed to free psychology from philosophical presuppositions which were preventing its development as an experimental science, but his original contributions to the emerging science of psychology involved bringing philosophy and biology together on a new basis which he hoped would eventuate in a synthesis of philosophic, biological, and psychic discoveries.

"A Plea for Psychology" was a reply to George Trumbull Ladd's attack on the **Principles,** which was published in the **Philosophical Review** and entitled "Psychology as So-called 'Natural Science.'"[7] Ladd's article was the occasion for the reply, but it is clear that in responding to him James is addressing the entire philosophic community. He asks hypothetically in one place, for instance, "Why should not Professor Ladd, why should not any 'transcendental philosopher,' be glad to help confirm and develop so beneficial a tendency as this?'" (CER, 322). He also characterizes scientists, both in the article and in the **Principles,** as having little "aptitude or fondness for general philosophy," nor, presumably, for anything which James, as a philosopher, would care to say to them (CER, 320). The intended audience was the philosophical community, which was understandably reluctant to relinquish even a part of its traditional subject matter, especially an area as cental as psychology. It is important to recognize the intended audience in order to clarify what they are being asked to forego and what they are being promised in its stead.

James sometimes uses the word 'philosophy' elliptically, to stand for 'transcendental philosophy' or 'philosophical idealism.' A particular set of characteristics, however, can be ascribed to 'philosophy' in the sense in which James at this time considers himself a philosopher. Philosophy in this broader sense treats questions "in their widest possible connections, amongst the objects of an ultimate critical review of all the elements of the world" (CER, 321-2). Its method is the Kantian one of showing how our experience of the material world, or any world, is possible (CER, 318). The goal of philosophy is "ultimate rationality" and typical questions of "ultimate philosophic grounds" are: "What the 'physical world' may be in itself, how 'states of mind' can exist at all, and exactly what 'taking cognizance' may imply" (CER, 318-327). Only in his later works does he reject this traditional philosophic rationalism, both idealist and empiricist varieties, with an explicit feeling of being relieved of a great burden. In direct contrast to the unlimited aspirations of philosophy, natural science is distinguished by its deliberate limitation of subject matter and goal, namely, that which leads to practical effectiveness. Science, as science, is necessarily limited ("a mere fragment of truth broken out from the whole mass") and thus employs unexamined assumptions (CER, 317). It seeks to find "definite 'laws' of sequence" built on such assumptions, rather than on first principles (CER, 318).

James argues that psychology should legitimately be considered a natural science, in principle, insofar as it takes as its subject matter that limited aspect of mentality which is wholly accounted for in our natural history. Of such temporal events, falling within the ordinary course of nature, psychology seeks the practical prediction and control which are the defining characteristics of a natural science. The biological study of human nature undertaken by psychologists, physiologists, and natural scienctists - even by psychical researchers - has yielded whatever promising new facts have been found in the psychology of the day. Rather than forcing such researchers to justify their findings on philosophic grounds, it would be more advantageous for the practical betterment of humanity to sharply differentiate psychology as a strict science, the proper sphere of "men of facts, of the laboratory workers and biologists," from "the more metaphysical aspects of human consciousness" (CER, 318-321). Although eventually philosophers should be able to take up the results of such scientific research and construct a rational, synthetic world-view, a premature imposition of such philosophical concepts as the soul or transcendental ego on psychology could only inhibit but not prevent the emergence of an independent science of psychology. More importantly, such an imposition would distort the understanding of those very "facts of experience" which philosophy needs if it is to avoid sterile speculation (CER, 320-323). James is both a Comtean positivist and a British empiricist in his insistence that theories emerge from, and are a generalization of, facts, and that disputes about first principles can only interfere with a 'harvest' of natural laws.

James sees his own original contribution to psychology in designating and arguing for an "undivided 'mental state'. . . as the fundamental datum" for the science of psychology (CER, 324). He thus shrewdly supports the birth of the new psychology as a positivist science by insisting on its limitation to observable temporal events, while undercutting its positivistic philosophy by designating a continuous, undivided mental state as its proper focus, rather than a series of disconnected sense data. Furthermore, he proposes developing a well defined and limited program of correlating such mental states with brain states. Thus, both philosophers and biologists can become psychologists, but only insofar as they each "forego ulterior inquiries" and provisionally take the mental state as the ultimate psychological datum. Scientific psychology should be free to develop unconstrained by philosophical presuppositions as long as it recognizes its own limitations and foreswears metaphysical pronouncements: "Psychology is a mere natural science, accepting certain terms uncritically as her data, and stopping short of metaphysical reconstruction" (PP, I, 141). One movement James hopes to counteract in scientific psychology by this disavowal of metaphysics is the reduction of mental states to physiological states.

James, then, wants to assist at the birth of psychology as a phenomenal science by clearing "metaphysical entanglements" from its path. Given this state of affairs, if forced to choose between a theoretical, philosophical psychology and a factual, scientific psychology, he would unhesitatingly choose the later on humanitarian, pragmatic grounds because science promises the most relief for suffering humanity. James, however, firmly believed that philosophers would have the last word, that, contrary to Comte, the limited understanding definitive of science will never be finally satisfactory, but will contribute to a more inclusive philosophic understanding of the world as world.[8]

Thus Reck's claim that in the **Principles** and **Briefer Course** James proposed a strict separation between science and metaphysics is well founded but needs to be qualified in light of all of James's early writings. It cannot be straightforwardly concluded that such a separation is either desireable or possible. The fact that James did not himself adhere to this strict separation in his psychological writings and that he afterwards explicitly repudiated such a possibility must be taken into account, especially in view of the reconstruction of James's larger project, as just stated. It should be recalled that, traditionally, psychology and metaphysics had been compatible, e.g., in scholasticism and Scottish common-sense philosophy, but with Darwinism, positivism, and the development of a mechanistic, laboratory-based psychology, the old synthesis no longer held. In supporting the new science James had to pronounce the old synthesis dead, but his intent was to prepare the way for a new union of psychology and philosophy, developed on a firmer foundation.

His view of the role of philosophy at this time is consistent with this interpretation of the relationship of philosophy or metaphysics, science, and psychology. Since he took positivism as the model of science, and rationalism as the model of metaphysics, each unalterably opposed to the other's presuppositions, his insistence on a clear separation which would avoid unproductive animosity must have seemed the better course of action. But James's own practice of psychology and philosophy already joined the experimental and humanistic disciplines in a unique synthesis which rendered such a rigid separation impossible. Unfortunately, he was not yet aware of the systematic possibilities of his own practice. Since the temptation is to read back (or make more explicit) the more original James into his psychological stage, it is important to recall this strict dichotomy between positivist science and rational psychology that framed his thinking about psychology.

James, like most philosophers before and since, understood philosophy as the task of seeking a reasoned basis for his beliefs. The purpose of reasoning is to lead to a satisfactory conclusion, passing from a state of restlessness or uncertainty to a calm acquiescence in the truth or vision of the good, a goal expressed long ago by Plato and Aristotle and in his own time by Emerson and Royce. Three versions of this final state attracted him because they embodied such an ideal of untroubled assurance, but also repelled him because they reached the end by a single leap, illegitimately, not having secured an unchallengeable warrant or justification. They are religious mysticism or poetic lyricism, philosophical idealism, and common-sense or ordinary understanding. Mystics and poets find "the peace of rationality" in which everything is explained, related, and made clear and simple "through ecstacy when logic fails," thus abolishing the opposition between knowing and being.[9] This is the goal stated in terms which seem to answer James's own deepest needs. But such a poetic, mystical goal could no longer be believed in solely on authoritative religious grounds or through merely artistic sentiment. The scientific temper of his time - and ours - is such that "one runs a better chance of being listened to to-day if one can quote Darwin and Helmholtz than if one can only quote Schleiermacher or Coleridge."[10] Although turning away from such mysticism as a satisfactory course of action in his early years, James nevertheless left open the possibility of raising it to a "systematised method."[11] However, he presciently quotes the eccentric mystic, Benjamin P. Blood: "The disease of Metaphysics vanishes in the fading of the question and not in the coming of an answer" (CER, 134-5, n.1). Towards the end of his life James identifies his own abandonment of the search for total rationality with Blood's mysticism, but, ironically, only after decades spent developing a rationale for doing so![12]

Despite his frequent criticism of it, he was likewise attracted to the idealist philosophical goal. In 1885 he suspected that an "idealist escape from the quandary may be the best one for us all to take" (CER, 281). He himself could not take that path, but by the time of **A Pluralistic Universe** (1909), although he still objected to the systems and faulty foundations of Fechner, Royce, and Hegel, he also still allied himself with their idealist visions.[13] Furthermore, late nineteenth century idealism, like Scottish common-sense philosophy before it, in his day was the philosophical tradition explicitly defending the efficacy of human effort in shaping a world consistent with human dignity.

Common-sense attitudes differ from the other two states mentioned in not being an ultimate goal, but "a perfectly definite halting-place of thought."[14] Common sense is the provisional state **par excellence** in that it accepts the world as it appears, with no attempt to reconcile incongruities when the only way to reconcile them involves simply dismissing one horn of the dilemma. Like positivism, it refuses to examine its own assumptions, but unlike positivism, it does not turn this inadequacy into a dogma. By ruling out feeling as constituting "the 'unscientific' half of existence," scientists adopt a monistic reductionism which dismisses rather than grapples with the central problem of reconciling the totality of human experience (Cf. PP, I, 138). Common sense cannot theoretically construct such a synthesis either, but at least stubbornly insists on the multileveled richness of experience. It respectably "contents itself with the unreconciled contradiction, laughs when it can, and weeps when it must, and makes, in short, a practical compromise, without trying a theoretical solution."15 Although James is plainly sympathetic to the common-sense view, he thought of it as an uncontroversial place-holder for the human dimension of experience which would give way, in time, to a thorough-going metaphysical reconstruction (PP, I, 141).

Of the two philosophic drives which James identifies, (1) "consistency or unity of thought," also expressed as "unifying the chaos," and (2) securing an objective warrant for individual emotional ends, the second was clearly overriding and remained so throughout his life. The first, however, was also a motivating force during what, for convenience, I will call the psychological period, which ends in 1894-5 with the rejection of his cherished project of establishing a new psychology as an experiential foundation for a new philosophy.16 I do not think that James really rejected the project in its entirety, but he was forced to reconsider some dimensions of it. This early stage is the time period under consideration in this article. I date the second stage roughly from 1895 to 1908, when in the Hibbert lectures, published in 1909 as **A Pluralistic Universe,** he acknowledged overcoming a deep intellectual crisis by giving up rationalism.17 In this second stage he argued strenuously against the first philosophic drive, but only insofar as it was taken for the whole of philosophy. He did not himself abandon it. Only in the last period of his life did he explicitly reject a unified vision as one of the two proper goals of philosophy and commit himself to the pluralistic rejection of the fertility of a closed system. Even then, however, he did not totally reject the possibility of such a vision, as a hoped-for consummation, in the sense of the first of the three goals mentioned earlier, i.e., poetic ecstasy. What he finally abandoned, however, was the possibility of providing a philosophic rationale for such a vision. He felt a great sense of relief in being able to accept the mystical feeling of oneness with the universe - the ultimate goal of rationalism - without having to provide a rational justification of it. Philosophy would have to be satisfied, as

philosophy, with a piecemeal understanding of reality, irreducibly pluralistic.

Despite his early adoption of realism in the phenomenal sense (1) of
the impossibility of any one ultimate explanation which would exclude
explanations stemming from other interests and (2) of the ultimate opacity
of brute fact, his project through the middle years consisted in working
through philosophic problems, which precisely meant adopting the aes-
thetically pleasing intellectual style "to which philosophies owe their
being," namely, "the craving for a consistent completeness."[18] What dis-
tingushed James from avowed system builders was that he was content to lay
the groundwork on which others could erect a system true to actual experience. When he criticised system building he was criticising such
aberrations as premature closure, before all the relevant facts were
known, as well as conceiving the boundaries of systems too narrowly so
that some aspects of reality were illicitly rejected. It was not until the
final stage of his career that he abandoned the philosophic project as
heretofore understood, leaving the second philosophic drive - securing an
objective warrant for our needs - as the sole business of philosophers.

Given James's predilection for metaphysics before, during, and after
the **Principles,** and his antipathy for the anti-metaphysical bias of positivist science, it would be odd for him to be arguing for psychology as a
strict science were it not for the fact that he thought that only by
carefully restructuring the domain of science could he negate its denigra-
tion of metaphysical problems as unwarranted intrusions on non-scientific
subject matter. He clearly abhors the "mechanico-physical" scientists's
assumption of a "purposeless universe, in which all the things and qualities men love, **dulcissima mundi nomina,** are but illusions of our fancy"
(PP, II, 1260). Furthermore, positivism's denial of sentimental facts and
relations 'butchers' those very "aspects of phenomena which interest you
as a human being most" (PP, II, 1259-60). He gives as the reason for not
giving a **psychological** account of free will, for instance, the argument
that science "must be constantly reminded that her purposes are not the
only purposes, and that the order of uniform causation which she has use
for, and is therefore right in postulating, may be enveloped in a wider
order, on which she has no claims at all" (PP, II, 1179).

Since James was concerned to restrict the claims of science so that
metaphysics could be taken more seriously, why did he nonetheless spend so
much time, and take so much pride in, helping psychology become just such

a positivist science? Hints can be found in some of these early articles, written before the **Principles.** Positivism, like common-sense, occupies "a middle ground," and in its indifference to metaphysics, it can provide a neutral phenomenal basis on which a metaphysics more in touch with human experience can be constructed. He held that "all philosophic reflection is essentially skeptical at the start."[19] Common-sense and all living thought takes the world to be objectively as experienced. It is only in reflection and dissection of such spontaneous thought that doubt enters in. In trying to reduce this reflectively generated uncertainty philosophers seek a better basis for belief. But new reflections can always undermine any such foundational absolute and escape from endless quandaries can be had only by 'stopping the play' and "assuming something for true, pass on to a life of action based on that."[20] Positivism represented such a refusal to question its own foundations and so could be used, not as a firm foundation to be sure, but as a point of departure, a descriptive beginning anew, in order to exorcise the endless search for foundations.

    In "The Sentiment of Rationality" (1879) it is apparent that empiricism, too, is congenial to James for the same reason. In acknowledging its inability to provide a grounding in "Nonentity" for "Being," empiricism simply accepts existence as a brute fact and refuses to pry into the mystery of Being.[21] In fact, this is its saving grace. Idealist philosophers, more ambitious in their aims, seek to ground theoretically the rationality of the universe. The most thorough-going attempt, the Hegelian dialectical linking of Nonentity and Being, has not succeeded but leaves the grounding of Being as opaque as ever. "Positivism takes a middle ground, and with a certain consciousness of the beyond, abruptly refuses by an inhibitory action of the will to think any further, stamps the ground and says, 'Physics, I espouse thee! for better or worse, be thou my absolute!'"[22] Positivism is a middle ground in its refusal to take a leap into a metaphysical absolute which prematurely achieves its grounding of Being by the simple expedient of refusing to adequately consider the possibility of non-being. It shares this modest stance with empiricism. But in its prohibition of the task of grounding Being, in its stubborn acceptance of the atomistic particles of physics as the only ultimate ground rationally defensible, it shares with idealist philosophy an unwarranted acquiescence in an absolute (albeit a physical rather than ideal limit) that itself needs justification.

Although commentators rightly stress James's sympathetic preference for empiricism, in the light of which his tolerance for positivism is explicable as challenging idealist absolutism, he viewed this refusal to rest in a false absolutism as but a stage in the quest for ultimate meaning. His life-long admiration for Renouvier and Hodgson, for instance, does not prevent him from criticizing their modest admissions that no account of experience as a whole can be given. Allying himself with the goal, if not the methods, of the idealist philosophers, he cannot reconcile himself with such a confession of impotence. Although it may well be that no satisfactory explanation of Being and non-being can be given, leaving mysticism as the only solace for ontologic wonder, the questing of ontologic speculation can only view such an outcome as a defeat, however emotionally satisfying such a leap of faith might be.[23]

In the second essay of the same title, "The Sentiment of Rationality," published (1882) a few years after the first, the practical and emotional motives which lead to philosophizing are explored, as complementing the theoretic impulse examined in the first.[24] They complement it precisely because, lacking any ultimate theoretic grounding which can legitimately exercise a veto over our actions, an account of warranted belief leading to appropriate action is especially needed. In an even earlier article (1876), anticipating his "will to believe" doctrine, he argues that the only way out of the theoretic dilemma of suspended judgment over the inability to provide an absolutely irrefutable proof for or against freedom or determinism, we must practically choose, nonetheless. No matter which theoretic attitude is adopted, the choice must be one in which "the entire nature of the man, intellectual, affective, and volitional, is. . . exhibited."[25] Speaking of Renouvier, he transparently expresses his own deepest predilections: "freedom thus carried into the very heart of our theoretic activity becomes the cornerstone of our author's philosophy."[26]

It is this most characteristic Jamesean insistence on slighting none of the interests of persons in either theory or practice that makes James's considered rejection of the possibility of excluding metaphysical considerations from the science of psychology a foregone conclusion. He says in 1895, speaking of the **Principles:** "I have become convinced since publishing that book that no conventional restrictions **can** keep metaphysical and so-called epistemological inquiries out of the psychology books."[27] What is difficult to understand is how he could ever have thought otherwise. In grappling with this issue some explanations have been put forward which have a bearing on James's philosophy as a unified project and which I think are worth pursuing further.

It should by now be clear that the identification of science with positivism and of metaphysics with speculative rationalism, joined with the historical circumstances surrounding the birth of psychology as a science from the womb of philosophy, led James to propose a strict separation of scientific psychology and philosophy. It should be equally obvious that this stricture would not, of course, apply either to the most lasting parts of his own psychology or to his evolving philosophy, the former not being positivistic and the latter not being speculative. In the same passage in which he repudiates the "child of my genius," i.e., his psychology, which was stubbornly functional, seeking thus to avoid metaphysical difficulties, he nonetheless defends the legitimacy of his 'offspring,' which has been misunderstood as well as despised. At the very moment of giving it up by repudiating the false dichotomy it was based on, he says: "My intention was a good one, and a natural science infinitely more complete than the psychologies we now possess could be written without abandoning its terms."[28] I suspect that the "infinitely more complete" psychology was actually written, or at least well begun insofar as one takes all of James's work as a unified project. In fact, he only abandoned the issue from the point of view of psychology as "a mere natural science," restricted to an uncritical acceptance of data, preferring to attack the same central problem - "the nature of that altogether unique kind of complexity in unity which mental states involve" - from the critical viewpoint "of metaphysical reconstruction."[29] A fascinating task, one well worth undertaking, would be to participate in reconstructing James's psychology, going beyond the text by making use of his own explicit philosophy, and in so doing, clarify the sense in which its terms should not be abandoned.

NOTES

1. Andrew J. Reck, "The Place of William James's **Principles of Psychology** in American Philosophy," Essay One above, p. 5.

2. William James, "The Religious Aspect of Philosophy," 1885, in **Collected Essays and Reviews** (New York: Russell and Russell, 1969, orig. 1920), p. 284. Abbreviated as CER.

3. William James, **The Principles of Psychology,** 3 vols., Frederick H. Burkhardt, ed., (Cambridge: Harvard University Press, 1981, orig. 1890), Vol.I, p. 263. Abbreviated as PP.

4. William James, **Psychology: Briefer Course** (New York: Collier Books, 1972, orig. 1892), p. 453.

5. William James, "A Plea for Psychology as a 'Natural Science,'" 1892, CER, pp. 316-327.

6. William James, "The Knowing of Things Together," 1895, CER, pp. 371-400.

7. George T. Ladd, "Psychology as So-Called 'Natural Science,'" **The Philosophical Review,** I (1892), pp. 24-53.

8. Cf., William James, "Clifford's 'Lectures and Essays,'" 1879, CER, pp. 140-1. "Now our Science tells our Faith that she is shameful ... in short, if we wish to keep in action, we have no resource but to clutch some one thing out of the chaos to serve as our hobby, and trust to our native blindness and mere animal spirits to make us indifferent to the loss of all the rest. Can the synthesis and reconciliation come? It would be as rash to despair of it as to swear to it in advance. But when it does come, whatever its specific character may be, it will necessarily have to be of the theoretic order, a result of deeper philosophic analysis and discrimination than has yet been made."

9. William James, "The Sentiment of Rationality," 1879, CER, pp. 133-4.

10. William James, "Reflex Action and Theism," 1881, **The Will to Believe,** Frederick H. Burkhardt, ed., (Cambridge: Harvard University Press, 1979, orig. 1897), p. 91. Abbreviated as WB.

11. "The Sentiment of Rationality," CER, p. 134. "Since the heart can thus wall out the ultimate irrationality which the head ascertains, the erection of its procedure into a systematised method would be a philosophic achievement of first-rate importance."

12. William James, "A Pluralistic Mystic," 1910, **Essays in Philosophy,** Frederick H. Burkhardt, ed., (Cambridge: Harvard University Press, 1978), pp. 172-90.

13. William James, **A Pluralistic Universe,** Frederick H. Burkhardt, ed., (Cambridge: Harvard University Press, 1977, orig. 1909), p. 94. "Fechner, Royce and Hegel seem on the truer path."

14. William James, "The Essence of Humanism," 1905, published in both **The Meaning of Truth,** Frederick H. Burkhardt, ed., (Cambridge: Harvard University Press, 1975, orig. 1909), p. 73, and **Essays in Radical Empiricism,** Frederick H. Burkhardt, ed., (Cambridge: Harvard University Press, 1976, orig. 1912), p. 100. For an analysis of common-sense in the **Principles,** see my "James's Reconstruction of Ordinary Experience," **Southern Journal of Philosophy,** XIX (Winter, 1981), pp. 499-515, and for his later works, see my "The Philosopher's 'License': William James and Common Sense," **Transactions of the Charles S. Peirce Society,** XIX (Summer, 1983), pp. 273-290.

15. William James, "German Pessimism," 1875, CER, p. 17.

16. "The Knowing of Things Together," pp. 399-400.

17. See Richard J. Bernstein's Introduction to PU, pp. xi-xxix.

18. "The Sentiment of Rationality," p. 115, and "Bain and Renouvier," 1876, CER, p. 28.

19. William James, "Lewes's 'Problems of Life and Mind,'" 1875, CER, p. 5.

20. Ibid., p. 10.

21. "The Sentiment of Rationality," pp. 128ff.

22. Ibid., pp. 127-9. W. V. O. Quine also 'stamps the ground' and stops at physical theory in **New York Review of Books,** 25 (November 23, 1978), p. 25.

23. "The Sentiment of Rationality," pp. 133ff.

24. WB, pp. 57-89.

25. "Bain and Renouvier," p. 32.

26. Ibid., p. 35.

27. "The Knowing of Things Together," p. 399.

28. Ibid.

29. Ibid., p. 400, and PP, I, p. 141.

ESSAY   FIVE

THE   "PRINCIPLES"   AS   A   HEARTIER

"ESSAY   CONCERNING   HUMAN   UNDERSTANDING"

Ignas K. Skrupskelis
University of South Carolina

In his **Essay** Locke undertakes to trace our ideas to their sources in sensation not only in order to demonstrate in detail that there are no innate ideas, but also to develop a philosophical method. The theory of the origin of ideas is to rescue philosophy from "vague and insignificant forms of speech, and abuse of language."[1] If his avowals are less explicit than Hume's, it is still true that for Locke the proper meaning of obscure ideas can always be established by discovering their sensational origins. I quote Locke: "the only sure way of making known the signification of the name of any simple idea, is, by presenting to his senses that subject which may produce it in his mind, and make him actually have the idea that word stands for."[2] In view of such strong claims, it is surprising how rarely Locke applies this technique to the vocabulary of philosophy. Rarely if at all does he present to our senses the sensational elements which give rise to the ideas of knowledge, truth, belief, the self, and the like.

Locke's treatment of solidity makes it clear that we need to obtain a distinct feeling, a unique quality, which in the case of solidity is noticeably different from feelings of hardness, warmth, or anything else. I quote: "If any one asks me, what this solidity is, I send him to his senses to inform him: let him put a flint or a foot-ball between his

The **Philosophical Psychology** of **William James,** edd. Michael H. DeArmey & Stephen Skousgaard, Copyright 1986, The Center for Advanced Research in Phenomenology, Inc. and co-published by arrangement with The University Press of America, Inc., Washington, D.C., U.S.A.

hands, and then endeavour to join them, and he will know."3 Furthermore, words cannot be substituted for the direct experience: "The simple ideas we have are such as experience teaches them to us; but if, beyond that, we endeavour by words to make them clearer in the mind, we shall succeed no better than if we went about to clear up the darkness of a blind man's mind by talking, and to discourse into him the ideas of light and colours."4 Locke's principles were better than his practice, for not-withstanding the impossibility, he employs words to explain knowledge, for example, as the perception of agreement and to claim that faith differs from knowledge by the absence of intuition.

In the **Principles of Psychology** James adopts Locke's program but carries it out in a much more thoroughgoing way than was done by Locke or his empiricist successors. As will be shown, James accepts the view that all ideas originate in sensation and attempts to clear up philosophical obscurities by paying attention to the appropriate sensations. The task of the present essay is to show that the **Principles** is the **Essay Concerning Human Understanding** written two hundred years later.

The intervening two hundred years are especially rich for physiology and psychology. As few other men James was in a position to summarize the new learning and apply it to the analysis of sensation, drawing upon every school and tradition and supplementing his reading with experimentation and self-observation. From his medical school days through the publication of the **Principles,** a period of more than twenty-five years, much of James's professional life was devoted to physiology. He read numerous journals; his books in the field are usually marked and annotated, many are author's gifts; he toured physiological laboratories; he planned and carried out experiments on his own. With as much interest and in as much detail James followed German physiological psychology and the abnormal psychology being developed by his French connections. Much of this he was aware of not only through publications, but also through conversations and exchanges of letters. And often James would rush off to check things out for himself. At least fifty times in the **Principles** James offers in evi-dence experiments undertaken by himself or assigned to students and obser-vations made upon members of his family or himself. The bulk of his work concerned sensation. This is true even of his often very time-consuming involvement with psychical research; time and time again his attention turns to anesthesia among trance mediums and questions concerning the sensitivity of hypnotic subjects. His restless mind, unable to carry out an experimental study to its completion, was quick to see that numerous seemingly unrelated lines of research could shed light upon the same problem.

At the same time, James was reading extensively the philosophical psychology of the British school, not only the usual Locke, Hume, and Bain, but also Hobbes, Reid, Thomas Brown, and the two Mills. He undertook to write the psychology in 1878. The twelve years of labor which followed overlap his teaching of the British empiricists at Harvard. In the academic year 1883-1884 he gave a course on Locke's **Essay,** Berkeley's **Principles** and **Theory of Vision,** and Hume's **Enquiry Concerning** Human Understanding. The same texts were used in 1884-1885 and 1885-1886. In the last appearance of the course, in 1887-1888, Reid's **Intellectual Powers** replace Locke's **Essay.** James's copies of these works are heavily marked and annotated, but most of the annotation was intended for classroom use. It should be added that James studied the physiology of Descartes and found Kant an important psychologist.

The present essay consists of two parts. In the first, I contrast the treatment of selected problems in Locke and James in order to demonstrate the much greater range of James's sensationalism. In the second, I discuss some of the developments in physiology and psychology which help us to understand why James often disagreed with Locke and succeeded where Locke had failed. The essay should contribute towards a general interpretation of the **Principles** as a synthetic work in which the traditional problems of empiricism are rethought in the light of the new sciences.

I

James does not explicitly announce acceptance of Locke's plan to treat obscure ideas by presenting to our senses "that subject which may produce" them. Locke's proposal is part of the background which is taken for granted. However, at least two texts from the **Principles** indicate that James accepts the general view that all thoughts begin with sensations. In one case he maintains that the lower centers of the nervous system react only to present stimuli, while the higher centers "act from **perceptions and considerations.**" He then proceeds to reduce everything to sensations:

> But what are perceptions but sensations grouped together? and what are considerations but expectations, in the fancy, of sensations

which will be felt one way or another according as action takes this
course or that? If I step aside on seeing a rattlesnake, from considering how dangerous an animal he is, the mental materials which
constitute my prudential reflection are images more or less vivid of
the movement of his head, of a sudden pain in my leg, of a state of
terror, a swelling of the limb. . . . But all these images are constructed out of my past experiences. They are **reproductions** of what I
have felt or witnessed. They are, in short, **remote** sensations.[5]

In the other case, while discussing the construction of space, he describes the kind of explanation to which psychology is restricted:

> . . . all the facts can be accounted for on the supposition that
> no other mental forces have been at work save those we find every-
> where else in psychology: sensibility, namely, for the data; and
> discrimination, association, memory, and choice for the rearrange-
> ments and combinations which they undergo (p. 806).

Obviously, such words could just as easily have been written by Locke, if
one overlooks James's reference to choice.

James's practice shows that for him also obscure ideas can be made
clearer by examination of their sensational origins. Time and time again
he simply points out the appropriate sensation and claims that clarification can go no further. This is what he does, for example, with the idea
of belief.

In James's introduction to his discussion of belief, he claims that
every mental state can be studied in two different ways: we can either
approach it by internal analysis and study the state itself to discover
the "sort of mind-stuff" out of which it is composed or we can describe
its relations to other states and conditions needed to produce it
(p. 913). Belief as a "psychic state" is a feeling which resembles the
emotions more than some other feelings do. The agitation of doubt ceases
and "an idea which is inwardly stable" fills the mind "to the exclusion of
contradictory ideas." It is in addition a state of readiness to act, a
"turning of our disposition." According to James the feelings of doubt and
inquiry are "like the emotion of belief itself, perfectly distinct, but
perfectly indescribable in words" (pp. 913-914). Having pointed out the
sensation in question, James concludes with the remark that "nothing more

can be said in the way of internal analysis" (p. 917) and goes on to consider the conditions of production.

It is the term 'assent' which in Locke corresponds to James's 'belief' because both are intended to include "every degree of assurance" (p. 913). In several passages Locke describes the conditions which produce assent; nowhere does he attempt to point it out as a unique feeling. Locke's claim that assent comes when one "has settled in his mind the clear and distinct ideas that these names stand for"[6] is like James's view of ideas filling the mind to the exclusion of all others. But Locke stops short and does not go on to say that there is a distinct feeling to be found. He misses another opportunity when contrasting faith and knowledge; the latter results from a series of intuitively evident steps, while "that which makes me believe, is something extraneous to the thing I believe."[7]

The problem of the perception of space also demonstrates the contrast between Locke and James. Although much too complex to be treated in detail, it presents several aspects important for the thesis of the present paper: after pages and pages of minute and technical discussion James ultimately rests his sensationalistic account of space upon the theory of the origin of ideas.

For Locke the idea of space is an intellectual construction based on data received through the senses of sight and touch.[8] However, he does not say explicitly just what those data are. Apparently, we are to consider the feelings of resistance when we attempt to penetrate the space occupied by another body. This experience provides us with the idea of filled space. The idea of empty space is derived by a kind of intellectual experiment; we can think of a body moving out of the space it occupies without thinking of another body replacing it. In this way, "the place it deserted gives us the idea of pure space without solidity, whereinto another body may enter."[9] In another place Locke declares that our complex idea of space is "made up" of simple ideas. Each of these is "'a sensible point,' meaning thereby the least particle of matter or space we can discern."[10] Had Locke gone on to say that this least particle is three-dimensional, his view would have been much like James's. As it is, Locke does not raise the question of the third dimension and it is difficult to see the bearing of his views for James's central problem. In the chapter on space, filled with historical references, James does not report Locke's view. Nevertheless, in his general criticisms of the associationist view of space, he often falls back upon Locke's theory of ideas.

James holds that there is a feeling of extensivity, a spatial quale, which is given in sensation. Without it, no intellectual construction of a three-dimensional space would be possible. The associationists, on the other hand, attempt to build up space out of feelings which themselves are not spatial. James argues that in this respect the associationistists are "heedless of their master Locke's precept, that the mind can frame unto itself no new simple idea" (pp. 900-901). He writes at greater length:

> The truth is that the English Associationist school, in trying to show how much their principle can accomplish, have altogether overshot the mark and espoused a kind of theory in respect to space-perception which the general tenor of their philosophy should lead them to abhor (pp. 901-902).

Those authors from whom James himself has derived the most "aid and comfort" "allow ample scope to that Experience which Berkeley's genius saw to be a present factor in all our visual acts. But they give Experience some grist to grind, which the **soi-disant** 'empiristic' school forgets to do" (p. 911).

With each of our sensations there comes a feeling which James calls voluminousness. This feeling is the **"original sensation of space,** out of which all the exact knowledge about space that we afterwards come to have is woven by processes of discrimination, association, and selection" (p. 777). We are apt to overlook it because rarely is there a practical reason to separate it from the sensations with which it is received. Nevertheless, voluminousness is felt by every sense: the sound of a thunderstorm is bigger than the sound of a squeeking pencil; the taste of roast beef is more extensive than the taste of vinegar; some odors are "bigger and rounder" than others. The same quality is received by sight and touch: "The interior of one's mouth-cavity feels larger when explored by the tongue than when looked at. The crater of a newly-extracted tooth, and the movements of a loose tooth in its socket, feel quite monstrous" (p.781). James is perfectly willing to pit his experiences in the dentist's chair against the whole **Critique of Pure Reason:**

> I call this view mythological, because I am conscious of no such Kantian machine-shop in my mind, and feel no call to disparage the powers of poor sensation in this merciless way. I have no intro-

spective experience of mentally producing or creating space. . . .
There is not one moment of passive inextensive sensation, succeeded
by another of active extensive perception, but the form I see is as
immediately felt as the color which fills it out (p. 905).

It should be added that James does not attribute definite dimensions to
this original feeling; there is at the start no distinction between surface and depth. It is simply the sensation of volume which is "indescribable except in terms of itself" (p. 778).

James's talent for finding unique feelings where others have found
merely intellectual operations is not exhausted with space but extends to
the whole field of relations. "We ought to say a feeling of **and**, a feeling
of **if**, a feeling of **but**, and a feeling of **by**, quite as readily as we say a
feeling of **blue** or a feeling of **cold** (p. 238). There is even a feeling of
absence, something very different from the absence of feeling, although
even the latter should be something which is felt. "And the gap of one
word does not feel like the gap of another, all empty of content as both
might seem necessarily to be when described as gaps" (p. 243), declares
James in reference to efforts to remember a forgotten name. We feel the
missing name as something "intensely active," rejecting candidates until
it itself appears. For James the several feelings of relation provide the
psychological support of the metaphysical theses of radical empiricism
about conjunctive and disjunctive relations. In the end, James's attack on
idealism rests on a psychological foundation. If only qualities and not
relations are given in sensation, souls and absolutes are needed to provide the connecting links. But when the psychological data are correctly
described, the sensational character of relations comes to be recognized
and no unexperienced connecting agents need be sought (pp. 237-238).

From James's perspective, Locke had announced his project premature-
ly: psychological observation was much too crude and imprecise to make its
completion possible. Locke at least had good intentions; his successors in
despair came to abandon as impossible much of Locke's empiricist programme
and thereby leave the field open for rationalism. The importance of the
new psychology for James's empiricism can be seen in the case of discrimination. Restricted by the available psychology, the older empiricists
could not appreciate the importance of discrimination and had to cut off
their analyses of sensation with the simple ideas of qualities. Modern

psychology shows that the suppposed simple ideas are not simple and that
the sensational stream contains much more besides.

What James calls discrimination is treated by Locke under the heading
of discerning. According to Locke, "discerning and distinguishing between
the several ideas" lies at the basis of much of our knowledge:

> [U]nless the mind had a distinct perception of different objects
> and their qualities, it would be capable of very little knowledge;
> though the bodies that affect us were as busy about us as they are
> now, and the mind were continually employed in thinking.[11]

The qualification surrounding this endorsement is in fact removed later
when Locke makes the perception of identity or diversity the first of the
four kinds of agreement or disagreement:

> It is the first act of the mind, when it has any sentiments or
> ideas at all, to perceive its ideas, and, so far as it perceives
> them, to know each what it is, and thereby also to perceive their
> difference, and that one is not another. This is so absolutely neces-
> sary, that without it there could be no knowledge, no reasoning, no
> imagination, no distinct thoughts at all.[12]

But Locke has little to say as to how discerning takes place. He says it
is the "first act of the mind" and speaks of the "natural power of perception and distinction." For Locke the "mind clearly and infallibly per-
ceives. . . all distinct ideas to disagree,"[13] but nowhere is it explained
how the infallible perception takes place. It would appear to be a purely
intellectual operation having no basis in sensation except, of course, for
the data being discriminated. The mind has two ideas present before it,
and without the assistance of anything sensational, it becomes immediately
aware that one is not the other. The difference is thought and not sensed;
nothing which can be called the feeling of difference is present.

At the beginning of his chapter on discrimination and comparison,
James quotes Locke on discerning at length and with approval. It is a fact
much to be regretted that Locke's

> . . . descendants have been slow to enter into the path whose
> fruitfulness was thus pointed out by their master, and have so

neglected the study of discrimination that one might almost say that the classic English psychologists have, as a school, hardly recognized it to exist. 'Association' has proved itself in their hands the one all-absorbing power of the mind (p. 458).

In fact, discrimination is as preponderant in mental life as is association. The very elements out of which associationism builds its world are themselves products of "discrimination carried to a high pitch," since in experience simple ideas standing by themselves are never found (p. 461). As has been seen in the case of space, according to James many different aspects can be discriminated in the ideas the empiricists claimed are simple.

Psychology in James's time was largely measurement of discriminative sensibility, the ability to notice changes in intensity of a signal. Many of the experiments involved the presentation of different signals in rapid succession. This is one of the developments in psychology which leads James to discover the feeling of difference. Another development is the study of successive contrast. It was found that the color and brightness of one object influences the perception of an object perceived immediately after, because after-images of the first object survive and mingle with the perception of the second (p. 662). Psychological information of this type leads James to declare that

> there is a real **sensation of difference**, aroused by the shock of transition from one perception to another which is unlike the first. This sensation of difference has its own peculiar quality, as difference, which remains sensible, no matter of what sort the terms may be, between which it obtains. It is, in short, one of those transitive feelings, or feelings of relation (pp. 468-469).

Whenever two objects are perceived in succession, the shock of difference is felt in the "brief instant of transition." The shock is furthermore felt as "taken up into the second term":

> It is obvious that the 'second term' of the mind in this case is not bald n, but a very complex object; and that the sequence is not simply first '**m**,' then '**difference**,' then 'n'; but first '**m**,' then 'difference,' then 'n-different-from-m' (p. 471).

It is clear that for Locke the order in which ideas are presented before the mind makes no difference to their felt character. As evidence one can cite Locke's account of how simple ideas are to be made clearer. He recognizes that even our simple ideas can be obscure. This is due either to a certain dullness of the organ of sense, or to the fact that the object made only a "slight and transient" impression, or to a weakness of memory which fails to retain the impression.[14] The obscurity can be cured by producing the same idea long enough and steadily enough to overcome the several handicaps. James recommends an entirely different procedure. Whenever the discrimination is uncertain because the difference is very slight, we can go back and forth from the one sensation to the other "repeatedly" until the discrimination is made (p. 471).

The shock of difference felt in the succession of sensations enables us to discriminate sensations presented simultaneously. This operation always depends upon the fact that the elements being discriminated have in the past been experienced in succession together with the shock of difference (p. 469). Otherwise we would remain blind to the complexity of the mental state and insist upon its simplicity. The same shock of difference underlies the intellectual operation of abstraction (pp. 477-478).

If for Locke discernment can take place without the feeling of difference, it is also the case that for him the idea of discerning itself has no sensational aspect. It is one of the ideas of reflection which the mind receives by observing its own operations, but the operation of discerning in no way feels different from other mental operations. The whole group of ideas of reflection will serve as the fourth and last illustration of the contrast between Locke and James. Once again James is able to find sensations where Locke could not.

For Locke, the mind having received ideas from external objects gets busy and watches itself at work. Such observation of mental operations is called reflection and gives rise to the ideas of "perception, thinking, doubting, believing, reasoning, knowing, willing, and all the different actings of our minds." Reflection, in fact, is very much like sense and would have been called "internal sense" had not the use of "sensation" in reference to external objects made such usage inconvenient. It should be noted that the operations observed through reflection in Locke are not always purely intellectual. Somewhat casually he remarks that our thoughts sometimes give rise to "satisfaction or uneasiness,"[15] and later, in order to show that the ideas of pleasure and pain are ideas both of sensation and reflection, he claims that "the thought or perception of the mind is simply so, or accompanied also with pleasure or pain, delight or trouble, call it how you please."16 But Locke is only making note of the connection between mental operations and pleasures and pains; he is not claiming that the latter are the "mind-stuff" out of which the ideas of reflection are composed. Locke provides definitions which describe the conditions of production; he has little to contribute towards the internal analysis of the ideas of reflection. His treatment of belief and knowledge, already alluded to, can be cited in evidence. Very similar is his discussion of volition. Many writers, he argues, confuse volition with similar acts of mind. But when to clear up such confusions we turn our "thoughts inwards upon what passes" in our minds, we discover only that the will is "that particular determination of the mind whereby, barely by a thought, the mind endeavours to give rise, continuation, or stop to any action which it takes to be in its power."17 Nothing is said as to what volition feels like.

James discusses the ideas of reflection in connection with the question whether or not we are aware of purely spiritual operations. In the chapter on the consciousness of self, he isolates what he calls the central part of the self and asks how this core of the self is "felt":

It may be all that Transcendentalists say it is, and all that Empiricists say it is into the bargain, but it is at any rate no **mere ens rationis**, cognized only in an intellectual way, and no **mere** summation of memories or **mere** sound of a word in our ears. It is something with which we also have direct sensible acquaintance, and which is as fully present at any moment of consciousness in which it **is** present, as in a whole lifetime of such moments (p. 286).

But just what is this feeling of the central self which Locke and the empiricists failed to notice? In the case of James himself at least,

the part of the innermost Self which is most vividly felt turns out to consist for the most part of a collection of cephalic movements of 'adjustments' which, for want of attention and reflection, usually fail to be perceived and classed as what they are; that over and above these there is an obscurer feeling of something more; but whether it be of fainter physiological processes, or of nothing objective at all, but rather of subjectivity as such, of thought become 'its own object,' must at present remain an open question (pp. 291-292).

Locke took it for granted that the existence of souls is a matter only of inference because souls cannot be felt. For him, there is nothing better than the vague idea of something we know not what which supports the mental operations.18 James, at least in the **Principles,** recognizes the possibility that the core of the self is a soul-substance, but would prefer that even this metaphysical question be settled by reference to what is actually felt.

All our mental operations, "attending, assenting, negating, making an effort, are felt as movements of something in the head" (p. 287). Each of these activities is felt as a unique colection of bodily sensations. For some of them, James claims, it is not a difficult matter to point out just which movements are involved. Guided by introspection, he proceeds to do this at considerable length in the case of attention.

When viewed in its intimate nature as composed of a certain kind of mind-stuff, attention is always found to combine the **"processes of sensorial adjustment and ideational preparation."** The former is always found in sensory attention:

> When we look or listen we accomodate our eyes and ears involuntarily, and we turn our head and body as well; when we taste or smell we adjust the tongue, lips, and respiration to the object. . . . The result is a more or less massive organic feeling that attention is going on (p. 411).

But even in intellectual attention, such bodily feelings are not absent. In James himself, they seem to appear as the feeling of an "actual rolling outwards and upwards of the eyeballs" (p. 412). It is possible to have attention without eye movement. We can train ourselves to notice objects in the margin of the field of vision. In such cases, attention is still felt, but now as the feeling of effort to form a clear idea of the object to be noticed. Such attention is felt as a strain (p. 415). For James the feeling of effort itself can be connected with a variety of bodily movements (p. 1105).

These examples show sufficiently how much more widely sensationalism ranges in James than it does in Locke. No doubt, James's greater success is due to the development of experimental psychology which for the rough introspective observations of Locke substituted a greater quantity of more precise data which, perhaps misunderstanding the character of the new psychology, James used as clues to more detailed and exact introspection. But the change between James and Locke consists of much more than this. Throughout the **Principles**, most of James's references to sensationalism are critical. He finds the sensationalists almost as bad as the intellectualists. The British empiricists failed to find feelings corresponding to relations and came to view experience like a stack of dominoes (p. 237) in which identical elements are recombined without themselves being in any way affected. The sensationalists did not understand that simple ideas are products of discrimination and are themselves never given as such (p. 219). They ignored the vague (p. 246), the feelings of direction, of tendency, the fringes which trail sensations. The two hundred years between Locke and James forced James to understand sensations in a different way. Two developments, the physiological doctrine of the summation of stimuli and the idea of organic sensation, made it impossible for James to be content with Locke's atomism.

II

James summarizes his opposition to British sensationalism in the notion of the stream of thought:

> What must be admitted is that the definite images of traditional psychology form but the very smallest part of our minds as they actually live. . . . Every definite image in the mind is steeped and dyed in the free water that flows round it. With it goes the sense of its relations, near and remote, the dying echo of whence it came to us, the dawning sense of whither it is to lead. The significance, the value, of the image is all in this halo or penumbra that surrounds and escorts it, - or rather that is fused into one with it and has become bone of its bone and flesh of its flesh (p. 246).

The doctrine of the summation of stimuli is one important source of James's criticism.

The facts were noticed by physiologists who were experimenting with the electrical irritation of various centers of the brain. A stimulus too weak to produce a response by itself does produce a response when it is rapidly repeated. Thus, the same result can be obtained either by using a stronger current or by the repeated application of a weaker current (p. 90). It follows that every stimulus of the brain leaves behind it some "latent activity" which fades away only gradually. As a result a subsequent stimulus finds a brain with "heightened irritability." In the brain, if they follow each other with sufficient rapidity, the several stimuli overlap each other. On its physiological side, attention too falls under the law of summation. Measurements of reaction time show that prior knowledge of the expected signal shortens reaction time: expectant attention raises the appropriate neural path to a "pitch of heightened irritability." Finding the path prepared, the neural current linking the stimulus and the response meets less resistance and traverses its path in less time (pp. 97, 410).

That every stimulus leaves the brain in a changed state is further supported by James's speculations about the wearing in of brain paths. Every current which passes through the nervous system must either follow an established path and thus deepen the groove or must jump a gap and begin the process of wearing in a new path (p. 112). In either case, the path of every subsequent current will be affected by the grooves which it finds.

The physiological facts are reflected in mental life in accordance with the law that every sensation corresponds to a brain state. Sensations also overlap each other exactly like the physiological stimuli. The precise character of every sensation depends upon the condition of the path which the corresponding current followed. Thus, no sensation reaches us in a pure form. Each one exists as part of a total mental state which includes the traces and influences of prior sensations. It follows that we can never have the same sensation twice. This would be possible only if the brain remained unchanged over a period of time (p. 227). In any case, the second sensation is bound to arise in a brain modified by the first.

The consequences of the physiology of summation for James's analysis of sensation are vast and lead to numerous criticisms of Locke and of the sensationalism of his school. Clearly, James's account of discrimination depends upon this fact: in the case of slight differences, unless summation took place, no amount of repetition could improve discrimination.

The same fact leads to the rejection of the view that all mental life is conscious life and of atomism in psychology.

For Locke, mental life is conscious because it is absurd to suppose that someone can think without perceiving that he thinks. With considerable scorn he rejects the Cartesian view that the soul is always thinking and insists that thought is not the essence but only an operation of the soul. How could the Cartesian view be true, he asks, in face of the fact that while sleeping men are as a rule unaware of any mental activity.19 It will not do to suppose that they think and immediately forget, for such thinking would be of no advantage to the soul. If having sensations falls under the general heading of thinking, it is impossible to have a sensation without being aware of the fact. James rejects such argumentation and for him much of what affects our mental life takes place below the level of consciousness.

Some signals of the sensational kind are too faint or last too brief a time to reach the threshold of consciousness. Yet they must leave some traces in the brain and affect subsequent mental states. If such faint signals were completely inefficacious, then no amount of repetition of them could produce a conscious mental state. Experiments with electrical currents show that this is exactly what takes place. Thus, it is clear that signals in themselves too faint must contribute to the distinctive character of the states which at last rise to consciousness. Every sensation has what James calls the fringe (p. 249), "this halo or penumbra that surrounds and escorts it."

Every sensation comes to us with a feeling of "whence it came to us" and "whither it is to lead." If the faint signals are viewed in physiological terms as giving rise to a tension which at last overcomes resistance,

there is no ground for supposing that the tensions whilst yet submaximal or outwardly ineffective, may not also have a share in determining the total consciousness present in the individual at the time. In later chapters we shall see abundant reason to suppose that they do have such a share, and that without their contribution the fringe of relations which is at every moment a vital ingredient of the mind's object, would not come to consciousness at all (p. 89).

It follows that the same mental state cannot occur twice and that there are no simple ideas which can be perceived over and over again. The color red perceived now is different from a red perceived at another time. Every sensation differs from its predecessors because every impulse follows other impulses with which it is intermingled. In fact, James is as much concerned with the "whither it is to lead" aspect which also surrounds every sensation. A sensation is always leading towards other mental states; it comes with a feeling of tendency. We expect it to be followed by other states and the feeling of expectation is part of the original sensation. As evidence, among other things, James cites the ability to read with appropriate modulations of voice texts which have not been read before (p. 245). Each word must come with expectations of other words which are to follow.

The fringe is connected by James with the feeling of rationality (p. 253). If in a train of ideas the transitions are smooth and the idea which comes next satisfies the initial expectations, the rationality of the whole train is felt as harmony. But should the fringes not fit together smoothly, we become perplexed and start looking around for other thoughts which should fit better. In this way the notion of the fringe permits us to correlate the physiology of summation with James's philosophical treatment of rationality. It also has affinities with the pragmatic account of factual truth as an ambulatory relation.

James holds that as a matter of habit much of the time we are inattentive to sensations as subjective facts. Their precise quality as feelings is usually of little interest. Sensations are important as stepping-stones of which we hardly need be conscious as long as they lead to the object we wish to handle (pp. 431, 488-489, 872-875). Sensations which are different can nevertheless lead to the same object, and it is the object which really interests us. As a result, usually we do not dwell upon a sensation and attempt to absorb its unique flavor. Still, the unnoticed aspects are quite active. They are in fact that gentle force which keeps our mental life flowing smoothly. When things go wrong, their absense or incongruity is felt as discord and uneasiness. From James's point of view, the empiricists were as inattentive as the rest of us and devised their mistaken theory of atomic sensations which can be felt over and over again.

Inattention to what does not interest us is also explained by the law of fusion. Sensations which come to us at the same time even through dif-

ferent senses fuse into a whole and it takes labor and effort to introduce
and maintain discriminations. The qualities to be distinguished must have
been felt separately at different times before they can be distinguished
when given together. Without the shock of difference we experience wholes
within which we are unable to make discriminations (p. 462). For James, it
is impossible to be certain that a sensation is really simple even when it
seems to be simple. The possibility of future discriminations can never be
ruled out.

Another very important idea leading to the rejection of atomism is
the idea of general sensibility which James owes to the physiology of the
nineteenth century. In James general sensibility functions as a Kantian
inner sense which envelops all sensations. Habitual inattention and the
law of fusion insure that most of the time the feelings of the general
sensibility remain unnoticed, although quite active.

The organs of sensation in Locke are the five senses and reflection
or the inner sense. But introspection shows that not all data of a sensational kind reach us through one or several of the six channels. Head-
aches, muscular strains, feelings of exhaustion are certainly felt but are
neither seen, nor heard, nor tasted, nor smelled, nor touched; neither are
they operations of the mind available through reflection. Where feelings
of pleasure and pain are concerned, Locke holds that they are available
both through sensation and reflection and at least usually accompany other
sensations. The wise creator has mingled feelings of delight or uneasiness
with many of our ideas in order to tell us what we should seek and what
avoid.20 And because Locke does not recognize that pleasures and pains can
be felt by themselves, he does not consider the possibility that men have
additional organs of sensation. On the whole British philosophy seems to
have accepted Locke's listing to the time of Alexander Bain and the publication of **The Senses and the Intellect** in 1855.21 Bain begins the study of
sensation with accounts of muscular and organic feelings.

The idea of the muscle sense was introduced by Charles Bell, while a
similar notion of general or common sensibility was developed by Ernst
Heinrich Weber, both in the first half of the nineteenth century. In **The
Senses and the Intellect,** without citing sources, Bain declares that the
muscle sense is now generally recognized as a distinct sixth sense. Sensations from this source must be discussed separately. The muscle sense
provides us with feelings connected with muscular action and with feelings
of the **"various modes of tension of the moving organs."** Knowing whether

our muscles are tense or relaxed, whether moving quickly or slowly, we can
judge the "positions of our active members." Bain notes that "these are
the feelings of muscle that enter most directly into our intelligence;
having little of the character of mere Feeling, and a very large reference
to Thought, they deserve a separate treatment."22

James recognizes the existence of the muscle sense but is less im-
pressed with its importance. It is a mistake, he argues, to consider it
the primary organ of space perception as many have done (p. 838). In its
place, however, he suggests other feelings belonging to the general sensibility. Recent physiological investigations show that awareness of spatial
position is primarily due to feelings in the joints.

The surfaces of knees, elbows, finger joints, are peculiarly sensitive, although the feelings which originate there are rarely noticed by
themselves. Much of the time such feelings are of slight interest; after
all, we move our limbs not for the sake of the sensations but in order to
see or handle objects (p. 830). But the feelings are quite active and
important. They serve as clues in the construction of perceptual space.
James writes:

> The joint-spaces serve so admirably as signs because of their
> capacity for **parallel variation** to all the peculiarities of external
> motion. There is not a direction in the real world nor a ratio of
> distance which cannot be matched by some direction or extent of
> joint-rotation (p. 830).

Feelings in the joints serve as a map on a smaller scale of "**a reality
which the imagination can identify at its pleasure with this or that
sensible extention simultaneously known in some other way**" (p. 831).

Sensation is as a rule accompanied by bodily movement. We turn our
bodies, raise our heads, focus our eyes, gesture with our hands and
fingers. Thus sensation is nearly always accompanied by feelings in the
joints of which we are largely unaware but which guide our judgments of
direction, position, and size. Thus, the qualities of outer objects cannot
reach us in their pure states, so to speak, but are always enveloped by
feelings originating in the body of the perceiver. James's account of the
central self can be invoked as further evidence that for him all sensations are accompanied by feelings originating in the body. The core of
the self is found where incoming sensations end and motor responses begin

(p. 285). As has been said, this center consists primarily of feelings of bodily movement which, James declares, remain "constant amid great fluctuations in the rest of the mind's content" (p. 289). The central core of feeling can be viewed as enveloping and mingling with all incoming sensations.

In addition to the muscular sensations, Bain devotes a separate section to what he calls organic feelings, those feelings which accompany the organic functions of the body. They are quite numerous: pleasures and pains connected with muscular exercise, feelings of exhaustion, hunger, thirst, nausea, repletion, relief following evacuation of the bowels, internal warmth and cold, feelings connected with the "genito-urinary organs."[23] James gives no separate account of organic feelings. He uses the term at least once, when in connection with attention he remarks that the accomodation of sense organs in attention gives rise to a "more or less massive organic feeling that attention is going on." But references to the organic feelings themselves appear throughout the Principles and play prominent roles in some of his most distinctive theories.

Organic feelings are important in his account of the identity of the self. A given stream of thought knows which thoughts belong to it and which do not. The criterion is a feeling of warmth and intimacy which accompanies some thoughts and not others (p. 314). Every thought belonging to a particular stream is branded by a feeling of intimacy and is thereby recognized to belong to that stream. James himself uses the image of a branded herd of cattle (pp. 319-320). But at least in part the feelings of warmth and intimacy consist of organic feelings. Their existence makes it possible for James to remain faithful to his sensationalism even in the case of personal identity. He writes:

> Our remoter spiritual, material, and social selves, so far as they are realized, come also with a glow and a warmth; for the thought of them infallibly brings some degree of organic emotion in the shape of quickened heart-beats, oppressed breathing, or some other alteration, even though it be a slight one, in the general bodily tone (p. 316).

Somewhat later, while noting that even the central core of the self is constantly changing, he again returns to the organic feelings:

> The central part of the **me** is the feeling of the body and of the adjustment in the head; and in the feeling of the body should be included that of the general emotional tones and tendencies, for at bottom these are but the habits in which organic activities and sensibilaities run. Well, from infancy to old age, this assemblage of feelings, most constant of all, is yet a prey to slow mutation. (p. 351)

The organic feelings, like all feelings for James, never recur. However, there is enough resemblance between them to provide a constant sense of identity. The various states in a mental stream are recognized by a self as its own because the barely noticed feelings of the self overlay every sensation.

I think it can be argued that in the end for James it is the whole body which is the organ of sensation. There are no simple sensations belonging to just one sense, but everything is received by a particular body in a particular state and this same state will never recur. The whole body with its mass of feelings appears to perform the function of Kant's inner sense. For Kant, all sensations take place in time because time as the form of inner sense is the form of all sensations. The unity of the self is realized in a stream of experiences standing together in one time order in accordance with necessary rules. In James it is the mass of bodily feelings which envelopes every sensation and brands it as belonging to one and the same consciousness. Where objective time order and spatial positions are concerned, James leaves room for intellectual construction. In opposition to Kant, however, he insists that many of the guiding clues are to be found in the given sensations themselves.

There is some tendency in James to see Kant and the later idealists as parasites exploiting the weaknesses of traditional empiricism. Kant's machine-shop is unavoidable if Locke's inattentive analysis of sensation is left to stand. On the other hand, the correct analysis of sensation will turn even Kant into a source of helpful psychological insights. James believes that the times are ripe for the proper analysis because several converging lines of investigation in physiology and psychology force us to notice those aspects which we habitually overlook.

N O T E S

1. James's extensively annotated copy of An **Essay Concerning Human** Understanding (London: William Tegg, 1853) is preserved in the Houghton Library at Harvard. All references in the present essay are to this edition. The text is quoted from p.viii, "The Epistle to the Reader." All subsequent references will be made using the following format: page number (book, chapter, section).

2. p. 376 (III, 11, 14)

3. p. 70 (II, 4, 6)

4. p. 71 (II, 4, 6)

5. William James, **The Principles of Psychology**, 3 vols. (Cambridge, Mass: Harvard University Press, 1981), p. 32. All subsequent references will be made in the body of the text.

6. Locke, p. 16 (I, 2, 16)

7. p. 501 (IV, 15, 3)

8. p. 99 (II, 13, 2)

9. p. 69 (II, 4, 3)

10. p. 124 (II, 15, 9)

11. p. 91 (II, 11, 1)

12. p. 382 (IV, 1, 4)

13. pp. 382-383 IV, 1, 4)

14. p. 260 (II, 29, 3)

15. p. 54 (II, 1, 4)

16. p. 144 (II, 20, 1)

17. p. 158 (II, 21, 30)

18. p. 189 (II, 23, 5)

19. pp. 56-57 (II, 1, 10), 143 (II, 19, 4).

20. p. 72 (II, 7, 3)

21. Alexander Bain, **The Senses and the** Intellect, 3rd ed. (London: Longmans, Green, 1868). James's copy of this edition is preserved at Houghton.

22. Bain, pp. 59-75

23. p. 102

E S S A Y   S I X

A S S O C I A T I O N

A N D

T H E   S E N S E   O F   S A M E N E S S

I N

J A M E S ' S   " P R I N C I P L E S   O F   P S Y C H O L O G Y "

Richard Cobb-Stevens
Boston College

> How comes it. . . that the logical relations among things should form such a mighty engine for dealing with the facts of life? . . . It is a very peculiar world, and plays right into logic's hands.[1]

William James often expresses astonishment at the fact that our conceptual network, which is ruled by the principle of sameness (or identity), should be so efficacious an instrument in our dealings with the realm of particulars, where sameness does not exist. Perceptual experience reveals that all particulars are unique, but nonetheless related by resemblance. Resemblances, according to James, are immediate and ultimate experiential givens, and therefore not reducible to even partial identity.[2] Identity is an ideal construct achieved by imaginative extrapolation of resemblance ". this strong emphasis on the priority of resemblance, however, we also find

The Philosophical Psychology of William James, edd. Michael H. DeArmey & Stephen Skousgaard, Copyright 1986, The Center for Advanced Research in Phenomenology, Inc. and co-published by arrangment with The University Press of America, Inc., Washington, D.C., U.S.A.

passages that seem to commit James to the counter-thesis that an anticipation of sameness is a necessary foil for the appreciation of resemblance.
We shall see how his critique of British empiricism establishes that a
prior sense of sameness always guides the discernment of similarity among
particulars. Thus, as Wilshire's commentary on the **Principles** suggests,
James never adequately faced up to the following paradox: on the one hand,
the conceptual thrust towards sameness is the condition of perceptual
recognition; on the other hand, our conceptual repertoire is acquired only
gradually, and is grounded in the experience of resemblance among particu-
lars.3 I propose to reflect on this paradox by developing three themes:
(1) the relationship between physiological and teleological dimensions of
the associative process; (2) the difference between the anticipatory
status of sameness as a rule guiding the work of resemblance and the
thematic status of sameness within an acquired conceptual network; (3) the
complementarity of two modes of rationality - the repose and clarity of
conceptual objectification, and the tension and vagueness of perceptual
exploration. This final theme is the key to James's understanding of the
interplay between anticipatory sameness, emergent resemblance, and conceptual system. Although he frequently comments on the tentative character of
all rational explanation, and emphasizes the ultimate opacity and mystery
of being, James nevertheless remains committed to the task of taking the
"postulate of rationality" to its limits (II, 1269).4 However, he makes it
clear that human rationality includes both the conceptual system and the
vaster network of vague and inchoate affinities which emerge on the level
of perceptual acquaintance. I shall contend that his interpretation of the
reciprocity between conceptual sameness and perceptual resemblance makes
for a complex and balanced theory of rationality. The rule of sameness
guides one of the mind's great passions, the drive towards ever more lucid
and elegant theoretical systems; the work of resemblance satisfies the
mind's "rival passion" for richness, complexity, and metaphorical
tension.5 These dimensions taken together constitute the complex network
of rationality, which is the locus where reality discloses both its clarity and its inexhaustible depth.

Part I: Association by Contiguity and Resemblance

British empiricism generally describes the mind as an interior space
containing representations of reality. The "cabinet" of the mind is empty
and dark at birth, according to Locke, and the senses are windows which

gradually ". . . let in external visible resemblances, or ideas of things without."[6] The mind develops its more complex ideas by assembling into configurations those elementary impressions which habitually occur together. The perception of unified things, therefore, depends upon associative linkage of atomic impressions on the basis of contiguity. If a subsequent appearance of a single impression or cluster of impressions presents itself as similar to an earlier appearance, then association by resemblance triggers the reappearance of the latter in memory, and the mind registers the connection between the two. Thus, the original cognition of perceptual complexes requires association by contiguity, and the recognition of either single impressions or perceptual complexes requires association by resemblance.

James makes several criticisms of this theory. First, he observes that the empiricists conflate the status of mental processes and their objective correlates: ". . . Mill and the rest believe that a thought must be what it means, and mean what it **is**" (I, 446). This assumption is founded on the more basic misconception that sensations, percepts and concepts are proxies which stand for the realities that they are alleged to picture. These two premises taken together motivate the unsuccessful attempt to explain conceptual generality in terms of the condensation of particulars into a blurred general image. Confining himself at the outset to an analysis of sensation, James notes that sensations are simply not experienced as mental representations within the mind's closed interiority, but rather as functional processes involved in the presentations of things (I, 195; II, 657).[7] There is something wrong, therefore, with the description of mind as an enclosure cut off from reality, an inner space filled with representations of things. Secondly, James argues that the same sensation or associative configuration of sensations could never reappear before the footlights of consciousness, even if the mind could legitimately be construed as a theatre of representations, because every sensation and, indeed, every mental function is a unique non-repeatable event in an ever-changing flux of conscious life (I, 130). Thirdly, while he agrees with Mill and Berkeley that perception differs from sensation by reason of its richer associative complexity, he rejects the premise that the most primitive sensations are isolated atomic impressions. Although sensation presents simple qualities like 'hot,' 'painful,' 'rough,' it always presents these as parts of "sensible totals," and as qualities of objects: "The 'simple impression' of Hume, the 'simple idea' of Locke are both abstractions never realized in experience. Experience from the very first presents us with concreted objects, vaguely continuous with the rest of the world" (I, 461). James first introduces the distinction between "acquaintance" and "knowledge about" in order to clarify the relationship between sensation and perception. To strike up a preliminary acquaintance is to meet someone for the first time; to know about someone is to be aware of background, character, and interests, in short, to be able to situate that person within a network of meaning. Obviously, full "knowledge about" brings into play the work of conception, but perception is already a kind of "knowledge about" to the extent that it is always governed by a focus-fringe structure. Perception detaches individuals from a background, and hence also relates individuals to that background. Moreover, every perceptual object also appears within a context of temporal fringes: ". . . the echo of objects just past and the foretaste of those just to arrive" (I, 571). James notes that it is only by a process of abstraction that we may isolate and concentrate on a sphere of pure sensation. To the extent that such abstraction is possible, we might say that the function of sensation is to establish mere acquaintance (II, 652). In fact, however, the stages of acquaintance and "knowlege about" are inseparable, for all encounter takes place within spatial and temporal contexts. Thus, sensation and perception are inseparable moments that blend the passivity of encounter with the activity of anticipatory understanding.

Since we first experience "original sensible totals" which present "concreted objects," James stresses that the function of discrimination is just as primitive as that of association. The elements which associationism considers its original givens are actually products of discriminating attention to some features of a sensible total. The most fundamental form of discrimination is the differentiation of foreground from background; the precise isolation of a quality from its sensible total probably requires considerable experience, and is more akin to the abstractive mode of discrimination needed for conceptual operations (I, 468-480).

James's chapter on association further develops his general argument that British empiricism does not adequately distinguish mental processes from their objective correlates. He first points out the ambiguity of the traditional expression "association of ideas," noting that we ought rather to refer either to the association between objects of thought (when we mean the "effects" of the associative process) or to neural processes (when we mean the "causes" of the associative process) (I, 522). Next, he claims that association is fundamentally a physiological process governed by the law of contiguity: "When two elementary brain-processes have been active together or in immediate succession, one of them, on recurring, tends to propogate its excitement into the other" (I, 534). Having thus introduced the physiological dimension and the categories of cause and effect into the discussion, he then reminds the reader that experienced objects are correlates of "thoughts" (his general term for intentional processes), and that thoughts are guided by teleological motives. He does not attempt to explain how the causal dimension of brain-processes intersects with the motivational dimension of thought-processes, but simply observes that what we ordinarily mean by association is the product of ". 540). Apparently James's purpose in this passage is not so much to advance our understanding of the mind-body relationship, but rather to indicate the confusion of levels of discourse that plagues the theory of association. Even though we cannot explain the link between neural processes and corresponding thoughts, it seems legitimate enough to postulate that the contiguity of neural pathways has something to do with the sequence of consecutive thoughts, at least to the extent that the flow of thought is guided by automatic association rather than by interested discrimination. Hence, we may legitimately ascribe a causal function to the contiguity of neural paths. But to claim that the resemblance between impressions could cause us to associate objective properties is to indulge in an implicit contradiction. By construing an experienced objective relationship (resemblance) as an intra-mental relationship between ideas or impressions, while denying that the latter are ideas or impressions **of** anything, and tacitly postulating an experience **of** resemblance within the mind's interiority, empiricism secretly relies upon the distinction between mental processes and their objective correlates. For if the mind can register a resemblance between two impressions, that act of registration involves an awareness **of** something other than itself. Consciousness is always consciousness **of** objects, whether the objects be intra-mental or extra-mental. Thus, it makes no sense to claim that resemblance between impressions **causes** us to associate objects or properties of objects. To experience any kind of resemblance is already to experience something objective. And if the mind is capable of objective knowing, then why describe it in the first place as an isolated enclosure? Ever since Hobbes's rejection of final causality, British empiricism has attempted to suppress the absolute priority of consciousness by appealing to allegedly "scientific" explanations of the process of knowing. However, these expla-

nations always tacitly rely upon categories (e.g., contiguity and resemblance) which are derived from the immediate evidence of consciousness.

Although James often stresses that resemblance is ultimately a perceived objective relation, unfortunately he never refers to the priority
of experienced contiguity over the conceived contiguity that explains the
physiological process of association. By grounding association in contiguity of neural pathways without noting that only a prior experience of
objective contiguity could make it possible to conceive of patterns of
contiguity in the brain, James himself almost falls into the same category
mistake that he detects in British empiricism generally, i.e. the tendency
to look for causal explanations of experience while tacitly introducing
experienced structures into the explanatory process.

Part II: The Sense of Sameness

James sheds further light on the role of association by resemblance when
he points out that the perception of likeness is ". . . practically very
much bound up with that of difference" (I, 499). In order that things
should be noticed as different, they must as a rule have some commen-
surability, some characteristic in common. Indeed, what could it possibly
mean for one thing to be totally different from another? In a parallel
fashion, the perception of resemblance necessarily implies a concomitant
awareness of differences. James attributes the genesis of genera and
species to this interplay of resemblance and difference: "The faculty by
which we perceive the resemblance upon which genus is based, is just as
ultimate and inexplicable a mental endowment as that by which we perceive
the differences upon which the species depend" (I, 499). Note that James
says only that genera and species are "based" and "depend" on the associative process of resemblance and the discrimination of difference; he does
not claim that the work of resemblance/difference exhaustively explains
the emergence of these categories. He recognizes that the thematic grasp
of genera and species as conceptual identities also requires "a **conception**
of absolute sameness," but he insists that the latter plays no part in
explaining ". . . how we perceive likenesses between simple things" (I,
503). Recalling his claim that resemblance is an irreducible component of
experience, he criticizes the view that things owe their resemblance to
their absolute identity in one respect, along with an absolute non-identity in all other respects. He then adds enigmatically that this view might
be valid with regard to compounds, but that it breaks down as an explana-

tion of resemblance between simple impressions (I, 502). This passage occasioned a fascinating debate in the 1893 volume of Mind between James and his Hegelian contemporary, F. H. Bradley.[8] Bradley criticizes James's theory on several counts. First, he rejects James's reduction of the issue to a choice between: (a) an appeal to the irreducibly ultimate resemblance between simples, and (b) an explanation of resemblance as a combination of absolute identity and absolute non-identity. This description of the possible options presupposes both that the ultimate realities are atomic simples, and that compounds are composed of separable parts. Bradley's thesis is that resemblance is better explained by the interplay of the inseparable, though distinguishable, moments of identity and difference (83). Secondly, he suggests that James's opposition to his theory may be based on the misguided supposition that it requires that partial identity be explicitly recognized. Observing that we frequently experience resemblances without being able to specify the point of identity, he stresses that a vague sense of identity is still a "perceptible identity" (83). Commenting on James's claim that we can appreciate that several sensible qualities form an ordered series without being able to identify the ordered structure of the series, he asks: ". . . how can we have a consciousness of uniform direction if there is not some one element common to all the degrees" (84)? Indeed, what could we mean by more or less, if we understand it as more or less of **nothing**? Thirdly, he expresses surprise at James's reference to simple impressions, challenging him to exhibit a simplicity which is ". . . barely simple and not qualified, at all or in any way, by complexity" (86). Even if an impression had no internal complexity, it would have to be qualified by its relations to an environment. He then correctly notes that James himself elsewhere seems to hold the view that simple impressions are abstractions discriminated within more original totals. Finally, he asks James to respond to the following questions: (1) If the extreme degree of likeness (identity) eliminates all difference, then why call it likeness at all, after describing likeness and difference as inseparable correlates? (2) If identity is still somehow in tension with differences, then will an imperceptible difference do? (3) Moreover, if the abstractive work of conception totally isolates identity from all differences, then how is such an identity distinct (88)?

James's rebuttal is remarkable both for the clarity of his responses to some of the criticisms, and for the cavalier fashion in which he dismisses others. Bypassing Bradley's opening comments on the difference between separable and inseparable parts, he claims that the crucial issue is whether or not we will admit the existence among our mind's objects of which we perceive to be, although numerically distinct, yet **like** each other in various degrees and ways" (208). He agrees with Bradley that sometimes we later discover an exact point of resemblance between composite objects, which we originally grasped only as ". . . their likeness as vague wholes" (208). However, he submits that it is invalid to generalize from this experience, noting that there are cases where we rest with the immediate sense of resemblance. In a parallel passage from **Principles,** he mentions metaphors which please and instruct, while also baffling our powers of analysis, citing as an example the description of a certain family as having "blotting paper voices" (I, 548). He accuses Bradley of taking resemblance always as a problem to be resolved by some higher form of analytic discernment, and then suggests that the quest for the "point" of a resemblance, if pushed far enough, leads either to the Leibnizian notion of an infinite series of points encapsulated within points, or to the "mind-dust" theory, which explains resemblances and differences as products of the varying combinations of uniform infinitesmal particles (208).[9] Both of these objectionable alternatives may be avoided by postulating that, whatever may be the ultimate composition of the final elements of being, their resemblance/difference is an ultimate experiential given. This position is consistent with James's thesis in **Essays in Radical Empiricism** that the ultimate constituents of reality are interconnected by transitive relationships, and with his frequent claim that being is neither solidly one nor irremediably many, but something intermediate.[10] One senses in this emphasis on the ultimate character of resemblance/difference the deep reason for James's mistrust of Bradley's Hegelianism. Bradley's claim that resemblance is vague partial identity seemed to James to be linked to the view that logical rationality and reality fully coincide. Admitting that the passages from the **Principles,** which are quoted by Bradley, do carelessly assume that the elements under consideration are simple impressions, James dismisses the suggestion that this assumption is essential to his argument, and counters that his theory of "ultimate unmediated likeness" stands, whatever may be the final components of experience (209). He makes no response, however, to Bradley's telling remark that a simple impression would always be related to an environment, the very point which James himself makes in criticizing the traditional empiricist neglect of the focus-fringe structure of all experience.

In a final exchange, Bradley agrees with James's wry version of Occam's law: ". . . antinomies should not be multiplied beyond necessity" (210), but adds that, if the basic issue under debate is the problem of the One and the Many, he would reaffirm that it makes no sense to hold these primal metaphysical principles apart. James responds that Bradley's discourse twice abuses ordinary English usage. He first observes that the customary expression for an identity which cannot be abstracted from differences is "resemblance," and concludes that Bradley has not really been attacking his position all along, but has simply been repeating it in an obfuscating manner. Secondly, he suggests that since Bradley's identity cannot be abstracted from differences, it differs so radically from the self-sameness which the term 'identity' designates in logic that it is inappropriate to refer to such different phenomena by the same name. James adds that he has no objection to the traditional logical sense of identity, and reaffirms the ". . . practical and psychological necessity of the assumption that identical characters may be 'encapsulated' in things" (509). Bradley has the final word, assuring the reader that James does not deny identity in the one sense in which Bradley affirms it, for James seems prepared to maintain that ". . . where the point of sameness is not explicit, it does not exist" (510).

I shall confine myself to highlighting those aspects of this debate (which John McDermott calls ". . . one of the most significant and elegant disputes of the last hundred years") that contribute to a clarification of James's understanding of the role of identity.[11] I take it that James is right about two points: (1) resemblance is an ultimate and irreducible phenomenon; (2) Bradley's use of the term 'identity' differs radically from its sense in traditional logic. On the other hand, I take it that Bradley is correct about three points: (1) there can be no such thing as a simple impression, a point that James was ungracious not to concede; (2) James's distinction between simples and compounds composed of separable parts is not helpful in determining the status of resemblance, which seems to be a tensional sort of reality whose parts (if there be any) must be understood as inseparable moments of the whole; (3) James should not reserve the notion of identity or sameness only for the thematic constructs of conception, since vaguely appreciated sameness is still sameness, and does play a role in the achievement of resemblance.

I am convinced, moreover, that James tacitly accepts the validity of Bradley's three points. There is no doubt, of course, that overtly he refuses to ascribe any ontological status to sameness. Perception alone establishes contact with being, whereas conception generates identities which may help in dealing pragmatically with reality, but which are not structures encountered within reality. In other words, James seems to reject the thesis that conceptual meanings are grounded in ontological essences. Nevertheless, he does claim that the conceptual sphere is generated by extrapolation from the perceptual domain, and he clearly takes the perceptual process as a "presencing" rather than a "mirroring," since he insists that percepts **mean** something other than what they **are.** Moreover, as we have seen, perception is not a passive registration of givens, but a discriminating and interpretive encounter. Hence, it is already a form of "knowledge about" and as such involves an appreciation of **what** it is **that** it registers. James's claim that perception always involves some anticipatory understanding of the fringes about its focal topic also seems to suggest that perception is guided by vaguely appreciated identities. On this reading, we could explain how vaguely appreciated sameness guides the perceptual work of resemblance: in order to recognize similars we must be able to anticipate a classificatory limit within which a range of limitation is possible. Thus, the theory of perceptual fringes introduces a dimension of sameness into that zone where acquaintance and "knowledge about" are inseparably intertwined.12 Unfortunately, James does not further explain how the sense of sameness functions in perception. We are left wondering whether the guiding structures of sameness belong to the dimension of acquaintance or to that of interpretation. There are some indications, however, that James was moving towards a theory of essence that might get beyond this alternative. This tendency is particularly evident in his efforts to describe non-scientific modes of rationality. In a discussion of the constituents of genius, he first ascribes all of those characteristics which differentiate human beings from animals, i.e., metaphor, humor, irony and wonder, to what he calls "sagacity," or the ability to discern essentials (II, 968-983), and explains this capacity in terms of our superior powers of discrimination and association. He then distinguishes two types of sagacity. The analytic mind, which flourishes among scientists and philosophers, emphasizes precise discrimination of the "bond of identity" between cognate objects, whereas the intuitive mind, which predominates among poets and artists, is fertile in the perception of resemblances, but uninterested in "singling out" the bond: ". . . so **minds of genius may be divided into two sorts, those who notice the bond and those who merely obey it**" (II, 984). Neither of these modes of rationality is superior to the other, for what the intuitive geniuses are sagacious since both discern the essential, even though only the analytic genius renders it thematic by abstracting the ". . . particular character called up by the analogy" (II, 985). As an example of how the poetic mind functions in a highly "rational though not ratiocinative" manner, James observes that Othello's death speech gives an implicit logical unity to Shakespeare's play, a unity which the "dry critic" subsequently makes explicit by specifying the precise bond of identity that guided Shakespeare's pen in composing the speech. The artist's thought ". . . obeys a **nexus,** but cannot name it" (II, 988). In other words, an anticipatory sense of sameness rules the work of resemblance. Since discrimination is always intertwined with association, we may assume that this vague appreciation of a nexus is the correlate of an incipient discriminatory insight operative within poetic achievement. The analytic mind simply accentuates a discriminatory attitude which already functions in a subordinate fashion within the intuitive quest for resemblances. This emphasis on the continuity between perception and conception renders problematic James's tendency to describe conceptual identities as mere constructs. To the extent that conception continues a process already at work in perception, it would seem more appropriate to describe conceptual analysis as insight into ontological structures, rather than as the imposition of classificatory constructs. A later passage confirms and reinforces this interpretation. Speaking of the genesis of classificatory systems, James invites us to consider the following analogy: if a hundred different beings were created, each endowed with powers of memory and comparison, and if each were given a "magic-lantern show" that imprinted on their minds the same lot of sensations, and if after the show were terminated, they were given a long enough time for arrangement and classification, what results would occur? James's answer reveals the full extent of his rejection of traditional empiricism, despite his apparent return in this illustration to the Lockean metaphor, i.e., the mind as inner theatre. He contends that each of these beings would develop identical classificatory systems, because their powers of comparison would yield insight into the ". . . relation between the **inward natures** of the sensations," rather than merely register patterns dictated by the order of their succession (II, 1238). Thus, perceptual comparison is founded upon a discrimination of the inward nature of **what** is perceived. James seems reluctant, however, to subscribe to a theory of intellectual intuition. Insight into essences is not a straightforward acquaintance with inward natures that are somehow "out there," waiting to be seen by the mind's eye. Essences do not belong to the realm of things, but to the realm of appearing. They have status only as ingredients involved in the presentation of things. This does not mean that they must be considered as subjective constructs, for appearing is a presentation **of** things and not a display of representations within the inner theatre of the mind. If we understand the work of mind as the way in which reality appears, rather than as a subjective organization of inner impressions, then the essential structures involved in the presentation of things are neither subjective constructs nor objective idealities (ideal things-in-themselves). To perceive something, the perceiver must detach it from a background, take it as x or y, discriminate it, compare it, etc. In this way, there occurs an insight into the thing's inward nature. The detaching from a background, the taking-as, and the discrimination are not something other than the perception; they are the interpretative procedures that reveal the inward nature, and **hence** make it possible to see the thing. Perception is both acquaintance and knowledge about.

To the extent that perception puts into play discriminatory insight into inward natures, it seems appropriate to extend to perception a comment that James makes concerning conception. Noting that conceptual analysis functions exclusively for ends set by our interests, he observes that the appreciation of essences cannot be divorced from the means-ends structure of cognitional activity: ". . . the only meaning of essence is teleological and . . . classification and conception are purely teleological weapons of the mind" (II, 961).13 This subordination of essential insight to interest suggests a way of describing the status of essences with greater precision. When James refers to essences as "teleological weapons," he stresses their **operative** status as rule-like guides governing both the intuitive role of resemblance and the analytic role of discrimination. Both of these modes of rationality are guided by anticipatory appreciation of essences. The difference between the two is this: the analytic mode sets as its goal the task of closing the gap between anticipatory and thematic understanding, whereas the intuitive mode prefers the exploratory richness of resemblance to the clarity and repose of identity. When James refers to identities as ideal constructs, he emphasizes the **thematic** status of essences when they are isolated by abstractive techniques of discrimination and named as objects. After having been named and rendered thematic, an essential structure acquires a new operative status as a component in the conceptual repertoire. Thus, there are two senses in which essences function in a teleological manner: (1) as anticipatory structures guiding semantic innovation; and (2) as components of an already acquired conceptual network.

Part III: Two Complementary Modes of Rationality

We have stressed the continuity and working relationship between the conceptual network and the structures of perceptual experience. However, James also stresses the discontinuity between these two dimensions by calling attention to the heuristic character of all conceptual constructions: ". . . we **hope** to discover realities over which the network may be flung so that ideal and real may coincide" (II, 1258). It is almost as though some benevolent power guides our theoretical constructions, however, since they so often prove effective in dealing with the complexity of perceptual experience. James concludes that ". . . the inmost nature of reality is congenial to the powers you possess."14 Our analysis has established a twofold continuity between perception and conception, by emphasizing both the role of anticipatory sameness in ruling the work of perceptual resemblance and the subsequent abstraction of conceptual identities from perceptual resemblances. Had James recognized more explicitly the first form of continuity, he might have been inclined to describe the congeniality of mind and reality in a less extrinsic fashion. The inmost nature of reality is congenial to our powers because both the conceptual drive for sameness and the perceptual passion for resemblance are modes of reality's appearance. His failure to acknowledge more clearly the ontological status of the operative essences betrays his incomplete emancipation from the empiricist model for mind. Operative essences are not subjective mental constructs but the structures of appearing. On the other hand, James was right not to suppress the distinction between subjective and objective completely, for conceptual thought renders operative essences thematic and therefore objective. The theoretical subject develops conceptual systems with an eye to their subsequent operative role in guiding the further work of perceptual resemblance. A letter to Bradley, written several years after the debate in **Mind,** tries once again to spell out their different attitudes towards the status of identity. James first insists that he never intended to deny the role of sameness: '. . . it dawned on me later that you probably thought I was denying sameness (a Mill) while I was only defending likeness."15 Then, using the term 'feeling' as synonym for perception, he adds that conception yields truth only when it functions in tandem with perception:

Where the 'roads divide' I fall back on feeling to interpret conception by (just as conception has to interpret feeling) and get what seems to me the fullness of knowledge out of both: while you, loyal to the original rationalistic direction which turns its back on feeling to pursue understanding through ideas, never fall back, but continue beyond ideas . . . to the supra-relational absolute. . .[16]

Thus, James sees himself as maintaining a position that avoids both excessive rationalism and excessive suspicion of conceptual systems. Perhaps his emphasis on the surprising efficacy of constructive conceptual systems is more important today, for it may serve as a counter-balance to a contemporary tendency to deprecate the role of conceptual clarity. He recognizes that we are interested participants before we are theoretical spectators. Things first appear not as objects of theoretical investigation, but as paths or obstacles in a vast instrumental complex. Moreover, essences are not first given as "frictionless ideals," but as the vaguely anticipated structures that guide association by resemblance. No one has stressed more than James the need for ". . . the reinstatement of the vague to its proper place in our mental life" (I, 246). However, in addition to the vague and tensional rationality of perceptual exploration, there is also the rationality of conceptual precision and clarity. Conceptual objectification must also receive its proper philosophical emphasis and justification. James asserts firmly that there is a place for a rationality based on the notion of objects set over against a subject, and hence for a kind of thinking that requires distantiation and objectification rather than involvement and anticipatory comprehension. His claim that association and discrimination are equi-primordial suggests a way of coordinating the perceptual and conceptual networks of rationality in a balanced manner. Association is a function of mind that accounts for our participation in being; discrimination is a function of mind that accounts for reflective distantiation.[17] The two functions are complementary and inseparable. This is why we are neither totally submerged within context, nor capable of a totally detached or disinterested point of view. Over-emphasis on conceptual distantiation generates the illusion of the absolute spectator, or the attitude which James called "vicious intellectualism."[18] On the other hand, overemphasis on contextual constraint makes it impossible to explain the emergence of the philosophic voice that describes the structures of our practical involvement in the world. In this regard, we may recall that James grounds freedom in discriminatory attention (II, 1166). One of philosophy's tasks is to explain its own possibility; to do so is also to discover the union of participation and distantiation that is our freedom. For the questioning attitude that generates philosophy requires both the anticipatory comprehension that follows upon participation and the conceptual discrimination that follows upon reflective distantiation.

NOTES

1. William James, The Principles of Psychology. 3 vols. ed. Frederick Burkhardt and Fredson Bowers (Cambridge: Harvard University Press, 1981), II, 1246. All further references to the Principles will be incorporated within the text of this essay.

2. Wittgenstein expresses James's position succinctly: "If someone said: 'I do see a certain similarity, only I can't describe it', I should say: 'This itself characterizes your experience'." Ludwig Wittgenstein, The Blue and Brown Books: Preliminary Studies for the "Philosophical Investigations" (New York: Harper, 1958), p. 136.

3. Bruce Wilshire, William James and Phenomenology: A Study of the "Principles of Psychology" (Bloomington: Indiana University Press, 1968),, p. 122 and passim. See also Hans Linschoten, On the Way Toward a Phenomenological Psychology: The Psychology of William James. ed. Amedeo Georgi (Pittsburgh: Duquesne University Press, 1968), pp. 117-186.

4. See also "On Some Hegelianisms," in The Will to Believe, and Other Essays in Popular Philosophy. ed. Frederick Burkhardt and Fredson Bowers. Introduction by Edward H. Madden (Cambridge: Harvard University Press), p. 197. Although James rejects the idea that reality can be completely understood, he does not reject the goal of showing ". . . that the real is identical with the ideal." Though it can never be achieved, this goal is the ". . . mainspring of philosophic activity."

5. William James, "The Sentiment of Rationality," in The Will to Believe, op. cit., p.59. Although the opening paragraphs of this essay (pp.57-58) seem to identify rationality with the ease, peace and rest brought about by conceptual clarification, James immediately adds that complete ration-

ality must include the "blurred outlines . . . vague identifications . . . and concrete fullness" of perceptual acquaintance.

6. John Locke, An **Essay Concerning** Human **Understanding** (Oxford: Oxford University Press, 1894), Vol. I, p. 212 (Book I, ch. 11, ¼17).

7. See Ludwig Wittgenstein, **Philosophical Investigations.** 3rd edition (New York: Macmillan, 1970), p. 96e (½275): "Look at the blue of the sky and say to yourself 'How blue the sky is!' - When you do it spontaneously - without philosophical intentions - the idea never crosses your mind that this impression of colour belongs only to **you.**"

8. F. H. Bradley, "On Professor James' Doctrine of Simple Resemblance," and William James, "Mr. Bradley on Immediate Resemblance," **Mind** (1893), 83-88; 208-210; 366-369; 509-510. All further references to these discussions will be incorporated within the text of this essay. Bradley's comments are also reprinted in F. H. Bradley, **Collected Essays,** 2 vols. (Oxford: Clarendon Press, 1893), I, pp. 287-294, and James's comments are reprinted in William James, **Essays in Philosophy.** ed. Frederick Burkhardt and Fredson Bowers. Introduction by John J. McDermott (Cambridge: Harvard University Press), pp. 65-70.

9. See **Principles, op. cit.,** I, 466-467 for a further discussion of these alternatives.

10. William James, **Essays in Radical Empiricism.** ed. Frederick Burkhardt and Fredson Bowers. Introduction by John J. McDermott (Cambridge: Harvard University Press, 1976), pp. 23-37, and William James, A **Pluralistic Universe.** ed. Frederick Burkhardt and Fredson Bowers. Introduction by Richard J. Bernstein (Cambridge: Harvard University Press, 1979), **passim.**

11. **Essays in Philosophy, op. cit.,** xix.

12. See Richard Stevens, **James and Husserl: The Foundations of Meaning** (The Hague: Nijhoff, 1974), pp. 24-32.

13. See also "Reflex Action and Theism," in **The Will to Believe, op. cit.,** pp. 94-95.

14. "The Sentiment of Rationality," in **The Will to Believe, op. cit.,** p. 73.

15. J. C. Kenna, "Ten Unpublished Letters from William James, 1842-1910, to Francis Herbert Bradley, 1846-1924," **Mind** (1966), 326-7. In a final letter James expresses regret that he and Bradley never came to agreement on the topic and leaves it to ". . . the younger lot to adjudicate between us." 330.

16. Ibid., p. 326.

17. The notion of an interplay between participation and distantiation is taken from Paul Ricoeur, **The Rule of Metaphor,** trans. Robert Czerny, Kathleen McLaughlin and John Costello (Toronto: University of Toronto Press, 1975), pp. 312-3.

18. A **Pluralistic Universe, op. cit.,** p. 60.

ESSAY   SEVEN

THE   VALUE   OF   EXPERIENCE

AND

THE   EXPERIENCE   OF   VALUE

Shannon   McIntyre   Jordan
George   Mason   University

Although James does not develop an explicit axiology in his philosophical psychology, he does plant the seeds there for his later discussions of moral and religious value. The soil from which his axiologial fruit grows can be identified in James's conclusion to his exhaustive description of the experience of Self:

> all that is experienced is, strictly considered, objective; that this Objective falls asunder into two contrasted parts, one realized as 'Self,' the other as 'not-Self'; and that over and above these parts there is nothing save the fact that they are known, the fact of the stream of thought being there as the indispensible subjective condition of their being experienced at all.[1]

The stream of thought (or the horizon, or fringes of experience, or pure experience as it is variously called) is neither subjective nor objective, at least in the usual senses of these terms. In fact in the above quotation, James calls the "all" of experience, the stream of thought, the "Objective" which falls asunder into Self-consciousness, and non-Self -

The Philosophical Psychology of William James, edd. Michael H. DeArmey & Stephen Skousgaard, Copyright 1986, The Center for Advanced Research in Phenomenology, Inc. and co-published by arrangment with The University Press of America, Inc., Washington, D.C., U.S.A.

what consciousness is of; and in the very same sentence he calls the
stream of thought the "indispensible subjective condition" of Self and
non-Self being experienced. Although James cannot seem to settle on terms
here, his philosophical point should not be lost; and fortunately it has
not been lost on recent phenomenological readers of James's nascent "discovery" of intentionality.2 In the following discussion I shall use the
term "pure experience" to refer to that soil from which consciousness as
well as objects of consciousness arise.

My thesis will be that value erupts out of pure experience at the
same time as the object of consciousness and consciousness itself arise. I
maintain that the object is already an objective value as it emerges from
pure experience because its very emergence as an object of consciousness
is concomittant with the valuing act of consciousness. A metaphor which
rules James's thought from the early psychology to his later writings is
that an organism focuses on a topic from the field of experience; the
selection may be called "attention," "choice," or "selection" depending on
whether the discussion is epistemological or axiological. When an organism
selects a topic for attention valuation already occurs. The valuation does
not **create** the topic or object and consequently it does not bestow value
upon the object, rather it **selects** a topic **as valuable** from the flux. Of
course the selection is, as we shall see, a crucial element. The value and
the valuation emerge together just as object and thought do. In this
paper, I will discuss James's foundations of axiology, his theory of moral
value, and then the value of religious experience. A concluding point will
be James's axiological pluralism and tolerance.

Radical Empirical Foundations

Throughout his writings James consistently claims that his work is empirical, though only later writings exhibit the self-conscious naming of his
philosophy as "radical empiricism."3 His philosophy is empirical because
it requires that ideas and their meanings be tested against concrete
experiences, and it is radical because experience is conceived in a more
fundamental, indeed trans-atomistic, way than traditional British Empiricism. Any topic of experience is as legitimate as the next so long as it
effectively resides in experience; thus, experience, conceived radically,
accounts for the continuities, connections, and affectivities among
"facts" quite as much as the facts themselves. It is precisely out of this

radical empiricists's ground that James is able to insert value squarely within the empirical frame.

While he never allows any kind of transcendental ground, James consistently identifies a world of pure experience (in his **Principles of Psychology**) which embraces both subject and object, two aspects or functions of the **same phenomenon.**4 This noetico-noematic structure of experience is further illucidated by James's notion that the act of knowing is "a straightening of the tangle of our experience's immediate flux and sensible variety."5 This straightening activity or special grouping of the original plenum may be called the mind, i.e. an "attitude" or intentional stance in the world. While his early work in psychology stresses this selection by the organism for survival and well-being, his later essays stress the practical ends toward which consciousness aims. In any case, we see here the foundation of a value theory. Certain topics within the field of pure expeirence are **present-for** the individual thinker who identifies, selects, and declares them as useful, helpful, or satisfactory in the very act of thinking; thus, the emergence of pure experience into intentional relata, subject and object, is already a value-laden reality. Valuation occurs in the attitude which shapes items within the field of consciousness: when one assumes a scientific, an artistic, or a religious attitude toward the topics **present-for** consciousness, one has already demarcated a realm of discourse and thus proclaims a realm of value as appropriate for the situation.

But how does one determine the propriety of a valuation? James's most famous answer is the pragmatic truth-criterion.6 Perhaps both truth and value can best be understood within James's understanding of "meaning." Only that which has consequences in the concrete life of individuals is meaningful, and thus can be either true or good:

> There can **be** no difference that doesn't **make** a difference else-
> where - no difference in abstract truth that doesn't express itself
> in a difference in concrete fact and in conduct consequent upon fact,
> imposed on somebody, somehow, somewhere, and somewhen.7

If a metaphysical dispute has no direct practical consequence, no value in concrete life, then it is meaningless even for theoretical life, for philosophy; if only that which has value in concrete life is meaningful philosophy, then axiology is central and integral with all philosphy, that is, with all fundamental thinking.

Ideas are true when they point to genuine objects or actions; this "pointing" is an agreement between two parts of experience, not a correspondence of concept to independent fact. For radical empiricist philosophy, truth means that the subjective or noetic aspect of experience must agree **in action** with the objective or noematic aspect of experience, and both aspects or correlates are the same pure experience in two functions. Truth, then, is the accomodation of one aspect of experience with another. "The knowing [the accomodation of noetic to noematic aspects of experience] can only consist in passing smoothly towards them [objects] through the intermediary context that the world supplies."[8] This series of intermediary experiences linking the idea with actuality is the concrete relation, or nature, of pointing between subject and object; furthermore, the linking is acting successfully in a context. True ideas are not only instruments of action, but they are also useful, and hence good: "The true is the name of whatever proves itself to be good in a way of belief, and good, too, for definite, assignable reasons."[9]

These assignable reasons are that true ideas serve vital interests in the concrete lives of persons. This definition does not condemn "truth" to an untenable relativism, but it does point toward Jamesean pluralism - and this will be important for understanding his axiology. Any satisfying idea is not necessarily true, for truth requires "good assignable reasons." Those assignable reasons mitigate the **prima facie** subjectivism of pragmatic truth: James says "that ideas (which themselves are but parts of experience) become true just insofar as they help us to get into satisfactory relations with other parts of experience. . ."[10] The whole of experience, the context or situation of the individual vital interest of pure experience, delimits the arbitrary character of the true; at the same time, since truth must accord with individual vital interests or concrete values, pure experience must allow for a pluralistic universe of truths and values.

Moral Values

If truth is verified by action, and if we seldom if ever have sufficient evidence to warrant any action which may or may not lead to verification, then before the fact we necessarily act on **faith**, on a hope born of a choice to be optimistic about ideas and their consequences. But to so act on faith is already to bestow value on the terminus of that chosen action: this value means not only the working of an idea but also its **worth.** The series of experiences which validate a truth claim also must be worthwhile, i.e. worthy within the overall project of life; this I take to be at least a part of what James means when he says that "truth is a species of the good."[11]

The first value to be affirmed as worthwhile is life itself, and James's own concrete experience provides the basis for his philosophy.[12] In 1870, prior to writing his great philosophical psychology, James reports that he underwent an existential crisis of Kierkegaardian dimensions (he mentions the Danish philosopher though not by name!) Life has value, is meaningful, only if one is free, i.e. can make a difference in the world by acting on choices. A strong will to believe, to act, to strive for good requires the freedom to choose, to act, to exert effort; in other words, a moral posture presupposes a free being. However, we are not free unless we affirm our freedom; the very **idea** of freedom **becomes** real, becomes a **true** idea, only in the act of affirming it, of acting upon it. "In other words, our first act of freedom, if we are free, ought in all inward propriety to be to affirm that we are free."[13] Freedom is for James, quite existentially, simply a **fact** of one's choosing. Ultimately, the living of one's life **is** the value of it: one constitutes one's life as worthwhile by choosing value, and this is the constitution of value in lived experience, i.e. in pure experience. The value of human life erupts out of pure experience by choice, but not arbitrarily, as we shall see.

We are free to choose the value of our life because that choice helps us to live, but we cannot **prove,** scientifically or logically, the validity of that choice; thus, we can believe what is beneficial without sufficient intellectual evidence for this belief. James does not shrink from such a conclusion, although he agrees that in many circumstances, e.g. in scientific investigations as well as in mundane curiosity, it is best to withhold judgment until careful investigation yields satisfactory evidence. As long as life affords leisure in deciding, careful investigation should be undertaken; but life does not always afford such leisure.

Most often a moral choice is one upon which we cannot wait for all the evidence. A moral question, i.e. a choice over "what is good, or would be good if it did exist,"[14] exemplifies what James calls a **genuine option.** When we are confronted by choice of any kind it is between options which can be live or dead, forced or avoidable, momentous or trivial: "We may

call an option a **genuine** option when it is of the forced, living, and
momentous kind."[15] Moral choices are so very excruciating precisely because they are genuine, i.e. live because both alternatives have appeal
and merit, momentous because making the choice will issue into profound
consequences, and forced because the choice will not wait for leisurely
investigation. Moral choices are painful to make because proof is never
forthcoming until after the decision is made. In fact, moral value like
truth is verified only by human action.

While incapable of proof, moral decisions are not merely arbitrary,
for by acting upon moral choices we bring about changes in the world and
these consequences either verify or not the value of the decision. Although the value is created by the choice and its ensuing action, verification by consequence demands that experiences "fit in with" overall
experience. Moral values, like truths, must relate to the whole setting of
pure experience which is as much **given to** as it is **made by** human choice.
Value, thus, is a phenomenon of noetic-noematic structure: moral value is
relative to individual experience but it is **not** thereby arbitrary.

While arbitrariness is rejected on radically empirical grounds, James
vigorously advocates a pluralism of values based on the very same grounds:
"there can be no final truth in ethics any more than in physics, until the
last man has had his experience and said his say."[16] Further, just as the
scientist holds as an ideal the systematic unity of truths about the
entire cosmos, the moral philosopher holds as an ideal a systematic unity
of truths about the moral universe. Each person, in concrete life, plays
the role of the moral philosopher by trying to account for his moral
choices, or his created values. An individual moral being and moral philosophy thus will both try to "weave them _valuesÑ into the unity of a
stable system, and make of the world what one may call a genuine universe
from the ethical point of view."[17] The moral philosopher contributes this
ideal of a moral unity to axiology. Further, this philosophical contribution finds its grounding in pure experience. The ideal unity of value
resides on the horizon or fringes of experience; as it is approached by
choices of, and verification of specific concrete values, the unity of
values retreats again into the distance. The ideal on the fringes of pure
experience thus calls forth a continual process of valuation. No wonder,
then, that James consistently advocates toleration and pluralistic attitudes. In fact his one great moral maxim encapsulates his axiology:

There is but one unconditional commandment, which is that we should seek incessantly, with fear and trembling, so to vote and act as to bring about the very largest total universe of good which we can see.[18]

Religious Value

James's writings on religious values exhibit the curious mix of science and mystic feeling which characterizes his own life. This curious mix may well exhibit his insight that pure experience erupts into noetico-noematic value structure, for value as experienced religiously is subjective, but it is neither arbitrary nor without objective content. In short James implicitly develops a "phenomenology" of religious experience,[19] and his phenomenology makes a primary distinction between the psychological origin of religious experience and its worth or value. James's real contribution to the discussion of religion is precisely his description of concrete, personal religious experience as having the same objective content, or value, as "truth" or "good."[20] In other words, if the religious experienece, e.g., as theologically stated, the belief in God, makes an actual difference in concrete life and fits in with the whole of pure experience, then such experience is both valuable and valid.

In describing the essence of the religious experience, James finds that all religions, minus accidental or cultural differences, have two fundamental truths. First, there is an eternal perfection which is seen by religious consciousness in the personal form of God. Second, men are better off in their concrete lifes if they believe in this God. These affirmations of religious experience cannot be scientifically explained, for such an "attitude" of scientific explanation is inappropriate for understanding the "given" in religious experience. To deny the validity of religious experience on the basis that such evidence is not available necessarily prevents the good the religious expeirence may bring about if it is true. Such reasoning recalls James's example of the mountain climber on the cliff: one must first believe in order to actualize, to make true, that which is believed to be true. Echoes of Pascal are heard in James's willingness to bet on the truth of religious experience because it is the only chance to reap the benefits of faith. Religious belief not only creates the possibility of salvation, as in Pascal, but it also answers a definite human need which living men experience.

Now theism always stands ready with the most practically rational solution it is possible to conceive. Not an energy of our active nature to which it does not authentically appeal, not an emotion of which it does not normally and naturally release the springs. At a single stroke, it changes the dead blank **it** of the world into a living **thou,** with whom the whole man may have dealings.[21]

The concrete and **positive** effect of religious experience in life is thus no less than the transformation of the entirety of experience; the horizons of pure experience assume a **personal,** divine aspect for the believer. As with moral value, the value of religious experience **becomes real, is made true,** by the believer's choice or will to believe. It would seem that the pragmatic test is here working to validate the belief: with his whole world transformed into a living **thou,** the believer's concrete life is fuller, richer, happier.

But from whence the force and whither the content of the transforming religious experience? As the answer to this question unfolds, James's constant pluralistic metaphysics and axiology of tolerance are thrust into bold relief. In all religions James finds that the experience increases the individual believer's spiritual strength, grants a new life, and puts the believer in contact with a saving force outside himself. James says that the man of faith

becomes conscious that _hisÑ higher part is conterminous and continuous with a MORE of the same quality, which is operative in the universe outside of him, and which he can keep in working touch with, and in a fashion get on board of and save himself when all his lower being has gone to pieces in the wreck.[22]

The MORE in religious experience is ordinarily called God in religions. Further, James finds that this experience of the power outside oneself is the source of moral consciousness in oneself. Hence the belief in God makes men have greater moral responsibility, which in turn influences their actions, hence their lives and the world they help create. Pragmatically, belief in God is justified. While the something MORE of religious experience removes the content of the religious experience from mere "subjective affectivity," the **effect** of this higher part of the Self in contact with the MORE **is** personal. The experience in total embraces both the subject and the objective content. Although the experience merges into reality, that is into effective dimensions, only in the concrete life of the believer **by** the choice to believe, the concrete individual neither controls, nor conjurs up, nor has dominion over the content of his experience. God may be personal, but no person's belief is definitive.

God, however, according to James's philosophy, is the providence of the religious consciousness which is identified by and expressed in institutions. Of religious experience itself he concludes, "The only thing that it univocally testifies to is that we can experience union with something **larger** than ourselves and in that union find our greatest peace."[23] Religious experience, then, points to the same pluralism which all of James's philosophy does. There can be no room for religious dogmatism just as the dogmatism of ethical or metaphysical rationalism must be rejected. The many gods of the many religious experiences enjoy equal legitimacy according to their influence and effects in the lives of actual experiencers. It is as though James is telling us that we should affirm the Divine in our expriences, but at the same time remain careful not to fall into delimiting the experience with a conceptually - or more importantly, insitutionally - defined God.

Conclusion

Experience, for James, is the source for both value and fact. Subject and object, valuation and thing valued emerge from experience through selection by an organism, but the topic selected must successfully fit in with all of experience. Value is chosen, but not arbitrarily. While each "chooser" legitimates his own value, no choice is normative for all: A pluralistic universe demands moral and religious tolerance.

Our discussions have led us to these conclusions, for James developed a metaphysics of experience and a theory of knowledge which are inseparable from each other and from value theory. In this view of experience - which is the only legitimate data for philosophy - there is no room for an unbridgeable gap between values and facts, as was the case for empiricism prior to James's radical rethinking of the empirical grounds of philosophy. James's view thus provides a powerful counterbalance to contemporary philosophical trends which are so austere and technical as to abolish the claim experience has for philosophical allegiance.

NOTES

1. James, **The Principles of Psychology,** 3 vols., (Cambridge: Harvard University Press, 1981), I, p. 290.

2. Stephen Skousgaard, "The Phenomenology of William James's Philosophical Psychology." **Journal of the British Society for Phenomenology,** Vol. 7, No.2, pp. 86-95, May 1976. I wish to thank Skousgaard for pointing me toward the thoughts I develop in this paper and encouraging me to pursue this subject.

3. James, **Essays in** Radical **Empiricism** and A Pluralistic **Universe,** (E. P. Dutton and Co., New York, 1971), p. 25.

4. **Essays in** Radical **Empiricism and A Pluralistic Universe,** pp.xiv-xv. And Cf. "Tigers in India," **Pragmatism and the Meaning** of Truth (Cambridge: Harvard University Press, 1975), p. 202, where James says that the object "seen and the seeing of it are only two names for one indivisible fact which, properly named, is the **datum, the phenomenon,** or the **experience.**"

5. William James, **Pragmatism** (Meridan Books, Cleveland, 1955), pp. 118, 119.

6. Recently this Jamesian notion of "value" has been phenomenologically identified as "world-fact," see: Calvin O. Schrag, **Radical Reflection and the Origin of the** Human **Sciences** (West Lafayette: Purdue University Press, 1979).

7. **Pragmatism, op. cit.,** p. 45.

8. Ibid., p. 228.

9. Ibid., p. 59.

10. Ibid., p. 49.

11. Ibid., p. 59.

12. See Ralph Barton Perry, **The Thought and Character of William James,** 2 vols., (Boston: Beacon Press, 1935).

13. William James, **Essays on Faith and Morals** (Meridan Books, New York, 1962), p. 146.

14. Ibid., p. 53.

15. Ibid., p. 35.

16. Ibid., p. 184

17. Ibid., p. 185.

18. Ibid., p. 209.

19. James Edie, for one, has recognized this aspect of James's "descriptive psychology" approach to religion: "I find that the so-called 'phenomenologists of religion' (Van der Veuw, Wach, Otto, Eliade) have taken a title to themselves which very inexactly describes their program. . . , it seems a misnomer to call this [their work] phenomenology. James, on the contrary, did adopt an authentically phenomenological approach (without the title) and has had almost no successors in this endeavor up to the present moment." "William James and Phenomenology," **Review of Metaphysics,** Vol. XXIII, No. 3, p. 524.

20. The litmus test for any value is always pragmatic; thus James succinctly states: "Her [Philosophy] only test of probable truths is what works best in the way of leading us, what fits every part of life best and combines with the collectivity of experience's demands, nothing being omitted. If theological ideas should do this, if the notion of God, in particular, should prove to do it, how could pragmatism possibly deny God's existence? She could see no meaning in treating as "not true" a notion that was pragmatically so successful. What other kind of truth could there be, for her, than all this agreement with concrete reality?" **Pragmatism, op. cit.,** pp. 61-62.

21. "The Will to Believe" in **Essays on Faith and Morals,** op. cit., p. 127.

22. William James, **The Varieties** of Religious Experience (Menton Books, New York), p. 127.

23. Ibid., p. 395.

BIBLIOGRAPHY

ON

JAMES'S PSYCHOLOGY

Michael H. DeArmey
University of Southern Mississippi

The following list of references contains reviews, essays, books, and dissertations which focus upon William James's psychology in a substantial way, or upon topics directly relevant to his psychology, e.g., his essays in radical empiricism or the 'compounding of consciousness' in his later pluralism. Most of the references cited are in English, and no attempt has been made at completeness.

For an account of James's life, the reader is referred to Ralph Barton Perry's The Thought and Character of William James (2 vols.; Boston: Little, Brown and Company, 1935), which remains unsurpassed in all significant respects. The standard comprehensive bibliography on James is Ignas K. Skrupskelis, William James: A Reference Guide (Boston: G. K. Hall, 1976).

The primary sources for James's writings on psychology are:

I.--The Principles of Psychology

A.-The Principles of Psychology. 2 vols. New York: Henry Holt and Company, 1890.

B.-The Principles of Psychology. 2 vols. New York: Dover Publications, paperback, 1950.

C.-The Principles of Psychology. The Works of William James. 3 vols. Edited by Frederick H. Burkhardt, Fredson Bowers, and Ignas K. Skrupskelis. Introductions by Gerald E. Myers and Rand B. Evans. Cambridge, Mass.: Harvard University Press, 1981. This is the definitive critical edition of this work.

The Philosophical Psychology of William James, edd. Michael H. DeArmey & Stephen Skousgaard, Copyright 1986, The Center for Advanced Research in Phenomenology, Inc. and co-published by arrangement with The University Press of America, Inc., Washington, D.C., U.S.A.

Notices: American Spectator, 16 (1983), 12.
           American Journal of Psychology, 95 (1982), 510-511.
           Choice, 119 (1982), 821.
           Journal of the History of Philosophy, 21 (1983), 270.
           London Review of Books, 6 (1984), 9.
           Philosophy and Phenomenological Research, 44 (1983), 124-
           126.

II.--Psychology: Briefer Course.

   A.-Psychology: Briefer Course. New York: Henry Holt and Company,
      1892.

   B.-Psychology: Briefer Course. Riverside, New Jersey: Macmillan
      Publishing Company, 1961.

III.--Talks to Teachers on Psychology and to Students on Some of Life's
      Ideals.

   A.-Talks to Teachers on Psychology: and to Students on Some of Life's
      Ideals. New York: Henry Holt and Company, 1899.

   B.-Talks to Teachers on Psychology and to Students on Some of Life's
      Ideals. New York: Dover Publications, paperback, 1962.

   C.-Talks to Teachers on Psychology and to Students on Some of Life's
      Ideals. The Works of William James. Edited by Frederick H. Burkhardt,
      Fredson Bowers, and Ignas K. Skrupskelis. Cambridge, Mass.: Harvard
      University Press, 1983.

   Notices: American Journal of Psychology, 97 (1984), 470-471.
              Christian Century, 101 (1984), 1132.
              Religious Studies Review, 10 (1984), 261.

IV.-Essays in Psychology. The Works of William James. Edited by Frederick
    H. Burkhardt, Fredson Bowers, and Ignas K. Skrupskelis. Cambridge,
    Mass.: Harvard University Press, 1983.

   Notices: American Journal of Psychology, 97 (1984), 470-471.
              Choice, 21 (1984), 1675
              Christian Century, 101 (1984), 964.
              London Review of Books, 6 (1984), 9.

V.-Essays in Radical Empiricism

A.-**Essays in Radical Empiricism.** Edited by Ralph Barton Perry. New York: Longmans, Green and Company, 1912.

B.-**Essays in Radical Empiricism** and a Pluralistic Universe. Edited by Ralph Barton Perry, Introduction by Richard J. Bernstein. New York: E. P. Dutton and Company, paperback, 1971.

C.-**Essays in Radical Empiricism.** The Works of William James. Edited by Frederick H. Burkhardt, Fredson Bowers, and Ignas K. Skrupskelis. Cambridge, Mass.: Harvard University Press, 1976.

The papers of William James are deposited in Houghton Library at Harvard University. Documents of interest in the William James papers are drafts and notes for his Lowell Lectures on the brain and mind, and psychopathology, lecture notes for his classes on psychology, and drafts of essays on such topics as perception, Kant, panpsychism, self, and the pragmatic theory of possibility and necessity. Also on deposit at the Houghton Library are the letters of William James. The call number for the William James papers is bMS AM 1092.9.

There are also some letters authored by James which have a bearing on psychology on deposit at Beinecke Library at Yale University. Of some historical interest are the "Logs" (3 volumes) of the Putnam Camp where James began **The Principles of Psychology.** These are on deposit in the historical room of Keene Valley Public Library.

1 8 7 9

Cabot, James Elliot, "The Spatiale Quale - An Answer," **Journal of Speculative Philosophy,** XII, 199-204.

Hall, G. Stanley. "Philosophy in the United States," **Mind,** 4 (January), 89-105.

Renouvier, Charles, "De La Characteristique Intellectuelle de l'homme, d'apres M. Wm. James," **La Critique Philosophique,** 8me Annee 1879, 369-76, 394-7, 17-26, and 41-8.

1 8 8 1

Salter, William Mackintire.   "Dr. James on the Feeling of Effort," **The Unitarian Review**, XVI (December), 544-551.

1 8 8 4

Gurney, Edmund.   "'What is an Emotion?'" **Mind**, IX (July), 421-426.

Marshall, Henry Rutgers.   "'What is an Emotion?'" **Mind**, IX (October), 615-617.

1 8 8 7

Anon.   Notice of "The Laws of Habit" (1887), **Science**, IX (February 4), 104.

Anon.   Notice of "What is an Instinct?" (1887), **Science**, IX (March 18), 254.

1 8 8 8

Carus, Paul.   "Determinism and Free Will," **The Open Court**, II (April 12), 887-888.

Gizycki, Georg von.   "Determinism Versus Indeterminism. An Answer to Prof. William James," **The Open Court**, I (February 2), 729-734; (February 16), 758-762.

1 8 9 0

Anon.   Review of **The Principles of Psychology**, **The Popular Science Monthly**, XXXVIII (December), 272-275.

Anon.   Review of **The Principles of Psychology**, **Science**, XVI (October 10), 207-208.

1 8 9 1

Anon.   Review of **The Principles of Psychology**, **Harper's New Monthly Magazine**, LXXXIII (July), 314-316.

Baldwin, James Mark. "James' Principles of Psychology," Educational Review, I, 357-371.

Coupland, W. C. Review of The Principles of Psychology, The Academy, XXXIX (April 25), 396-397.

Hall, G. Stanley. Review of The Principles of Psychology, The American Journal of Psychology, III (February), 578-591.

Myers, Frederick W. H. Review of The Principles of Psychology, Proceedings of the Society for Physical Research (English), vol. VII, part XVIII (April), 111-133.

Peirce, Charles Sanders. Review of The Principles of Psychology, The Nation, LIII (July 2), 15; (July 29), 32-33.

Royce, Josiah. "A New Study of Psychology," The International Journal of Ethics, I (January), 143-169.

Santayana, George. Review of The Principles of Psychology, The Atlantic Monthly, LXVII (April), 552-556.

Sully, James. Review of The Principles of Psychology, Mind, XVI (July), 393-404.

1 8 9 2

Anon. Review of The Principles of Psychology, The Athenaeum, no. 3382 (August 20), 246-248.

Carus, Paul. "The Nature of Mind and the Meaning of Reality," The Philosophical Review, I (May) 299-305.

Gordy, J. P. "Professor Ladd's Criticism of James's Psychology," The Philosophical Review, I (January) 299-305.

Ladd, George Trumball. "Psychology as So-called 'Natural Science,'" The Philosophical Review, I (January) 24-53.

Marillier, Leon. "La Psychologie de William James," Revue Philosophique, XXXIV, 449-470; 603-627; XXXV, 1-32; 145-183.

Stanley, Hiram M. "Some Remarks Upon Professor James's Discussion of Attention," The Monist, III (October), 122-124.

Ward, James. Review of Psychology, Mind, NS I (October), 531-539.

Worcester, W. L. "Observations on Some Points in James's Psychology I, II, III," The Monist, April, 417-434; January, 1893; 285-298; October 1893, 129-143.

1 8 9 3

Bradley, F. H. "On Professor James's Doctrine of Simple Resemblance," Mind, NS II (January), 83-88. Reprinted in Collected Essays (1935).

Ford, E. "The Original Datum of Space-Consciousness," Mind, NS II (April), 217-218.

1 8 9 4

Baldwin, James M. "The Origin of Emotional Expression," The Psychological Review, I (November), 610-623.

Dewey, John. "The Theory of Emotion," The Psychological Review, I (November) 553-569; II (January 1895), 13-32.

Gardiner, Harry Norman. Review of literature on emotion, The Psychological Review, I (September) 544-551.

Irons, David. "Prof. James' Theory of Emotion," Mind, NS III (January), 77-97.

Ladd, George Trumbull. "Is Psychology a Science?" The Psychological Review, I (July), 392-395.

Sollier, Paul. "Recherches sur les rapports de la sensibilité et de l'emotion," Revue Philosophique, XXXVII, 241-266.

1 8 9 5

Baldwin, J. M., Cattell, J., Ladd, G. T., "Letters to the Editor,"

Science, N. S. 2 (November), 626-628.

Irons, David. "The Physical Basis of Emotion. A Reply," **Mind,** NS IV, 92-99.

1 8 9 6

Anon. Notice of "Is Life Worth Living?" (1895), The Dial, XX (June 16), 366.

Bryant, Sophie. "Professor James on the Emotions," **Proceedings of the Aristotelian Society,** vol. III, no. 2, 52-64.

Cattell, J. McKeen. Notice of "Address of the President before the Society for Psychical Research," **The Psychological Review,** III (September), 582-583.

Davidson, Thomas. "'Is Life Worth Living?'" **The International Journal of Ethics,** VI (January), 231-235.

Gardiner, Harry Norman. "Recent Discussion of Emotion," The Philosophical **Review,** V (January), 102-112.

1 8 9 8

Schiller, F. C. S. "Review of **Human Immortality,**" **The Nation,** LXVII (December 1), 416-417.

1 8 9 9

Anon. Notice of **Talks to Teachers,** The Dial, XXVII (October 16), 276.

Davidson, Thomas. Review of **Human** Immortality, **The International Journal of Ethics,** IX (January), 256-259.

DeGarmo, Charles. Review of **Talks to Teachers,** Science, NS IX (June 30), 909-910.

Griffen, Edward H. Review of **Talks to Teachers, The Psychological Review,** VI (September), 336-339.

Hodder, Alfred. Review of **Talks to Teachers, The Nation,** LXVIII (June

22), 481-482.

Hoge, C. W.   Review of **Human Immortality, The Philosophical Review,** VI (July), 424-426.

1 9 0 0

Pratt, Cornelia Atwood.   "Teachers, Students, and Professor James," **The Critic,** XXXVI (Fall), 119-121.

Sherrington, C. S.   "Experimentation on Emotion," **Nature,** LXII (August 2), 328-331.

_____.   "Experiments on the Value of Vascular and Visceral Factors for the Genesis of Emotion," **Proceedings of the Royal Society of London,** LXVI, 390-403.

1 9 0 1

Howison, George Holmes.   "Human Immortality: Its Positive Argument" in **The Limits of Evolution** and **Other Essays Illustrating the Metaphysical Theory of Personal Idealism.** New York: Macmillan.

Myers, Charles S.   "Experimentation on Emotion," **Mind,** NS X, 114-115.

1 9 0 5

Judd, Charles H.   "Radical Empiricism and Wundt's Philosophy," **The Journal of Philosophy,** II (March 30), 169-176.

Tower, C. V.   "A Neglected 'Context' in 'Radical Empiricism'," **The Journal of Philosophy,** II (July 20), 400-408.

Weigle, L. A.   Review of "Does 'Consciousness' Exist?" (1904) and "A World of Pure Experience" (1904), **The Psychological Bulletin,** II (March 15), 99-102.

1 9 0 6

Leighton, J. A.   "Cognitive Thought and 'Immediate' Experience," **The Journal of Philosophy** III (March 29), 174-180.

Nichols, Herbert.   "Professor James's 'Hole,'" **The Journal of Philosophy,**

III (February 1), 64-70.

Pitkin, Walter B. "A Problem of Evidence in Radical Empiricism," **The Journal of Philosophy,** III (November 22), 645-650.

Russell, John E. "Solipsism: The Logical Issue of Radical Empiricism," **The Philosophical Review,** XV (November), 606-613.

_____. "Some Difficulties with the Epistemology of Pragmatism and Radical Empiricism," **The Philosophical Review,** XV (July), 406-413.

1 9 0 7

McGilvary, Evander Bradley. "The Stream of Consciousness," **The Journal of Philosophy,** IV (April 25), 225-235.

Münsterberg, Hugo. "Professor James as a Psychologist," **The Harvard Illustrated Magazine,** VII (February), 97-98.

1 9 0 8

Witmer, Lightner. "Mental Healing and the Emmanuel Movement," **The Psychological Clinic,** II (December 15), 212-223; (January 15, 1909). 239-250; (February 15, 1909), 282-300.

1 9 0 9

Anon. "Is the Psychology Taught at Harvard a National Peril?" **Current Literature,** XLVI (April), 437-438.

Baudin, E. "La Methode Psychologique de W. James," Preface to **Précis de psychologie,** translated by E. Baudin and G. Bertier. Paris: Marcel Riviere.

Sanborn, Herbert C. **Über die Identität der Person bei William James.** Leipzig: Bohme & Lehmann.

Shargha, Ikbal Kishen. **Examination of Prof. William James's Psychology.** Allhabad, India: Ram Narain Lal.

Tausch, Edwin. "William James, The Pragmatismus - A Psychological Analysis," **The Monist,** XIX (January), 1-26.

Wodehouse, Helen. "Professor James on Conception," **The Journal of Philosophy,** VI (September 2), 490-495.

1 9 1 0

McDougal, William. "The Work of William James. II. As Psychologist," **The
Sociological Review,** III, 314-315.

Menard, Alphonse. **Analyse et critique des principes de la psychologie de
W. James.** Lyon: Imprimeries reunies.

Miller, Dickinson S. "Some of the Tendiences of Professor James's Work,"
The Journal of Philosophy, VII (November 24), 645-664.

Ruttmann, W. J. "Die Hauptpunkte der Jamesschen Psychologie," **Die deutsche
Schule,** XIV, 751-757.

1 9 1 1

Angell, James Rowland. "William James," **The Psychological Review,** XVIII
(January), 78-82.

Bocker, Theodor. **Die James-Lange'sche Gefuhlstheorie in ihrer historischen
Entwicklung.** Leipzig: Breitkopf & Hartel.

Cook, Helen D. "The James-Lange Theory of the Emotions and the Sensationalistic Analysis of Thinking," **The Psychological Bulletin,** VIII
(March 15), 101-106.

McGilvary, E. G. "The Fringe in William James's Psychology: The Basis of
Logic." **The Philosophical Review,** 20, 137-164.

Riley, Isaac Woodbridge. "Continental Critics of Pragmatism," **The Journal
of Philosophy,** VIII (April 27), 225-232; (May 25), 289-294.

Royce, Josiah. "William James and the Philosophy of Life" in **William James
and Other Essays on the Philosophy of Life.** New York: Macmillan. Also
appeared in **Science,** XXXIV (July 14), 33-45; **Harvard Graduates'
Magazine,** XX (1911-1912), 1-18; **The Boston Evening Transcript,** June
29, 1911, p. 13.

Wundt, Wilhelm. **Probleme der Volkerpsychologie.** Leipzig: Ernst Wiegandt.

1 9 1 2

Boutroux, Émile. **William James.** London: Longmans, Green.

Russell, Bertrand. Review of **Essays in Radical Empiricism, Mind,** NS XXI
(October), 571-575.

1 9 1 3

Bush, Wendell T. "The Empiricism of James," The Journal of Philosophy, X
(September 25), 533-541.

Knox, Howard V. "William James and His Philosophy," **Mind,** NS XXII
(April), 231-242.

Reverdin, Henri. **La Notion d'experience d'apres William James.** Geneva:
Georg et Co.

Schiller, F. C. S. Review of R. B. Perry, **Present Philosophical Tendencies** (1912), **Mind,** NS XXII (April), 280-284.

1 9 1 4

Bradley, Francis Herbert. **Essays on Truth and Reality.** Oxford: Clarendon.

Kallen, Horace M. **William James and Henri Bergson: A Study of Contrasting
Theories of Life.** Chicago: University of Chicago Press.

_____. Review of H. Reverdin, **La Notion d'experience d'apres
William James** (1913), The Philosophical Review, XXIII (May), 357-359.

Knox, Howard V. **The Philosophy of William James.** London: Constable.

_____. Review of H. Reverdin, **La Notion d'experience d'apres William
James** (1913), Mind, NS XXIII (October), 604-608.

Stebbing, L. Susan. **Pragmatism and French Voluntarism.** Cambridge, England:
At the University Press.

Titchner, Edward Bradford. "An Historical Note on the James-Lange Theory
of Emotion," The American Journal of Psychology, XXV (July), 427-447.

Vogt, P. B.   "From John Stuart Mill to William James," **The Catholic University Bulletin,** XX (February), 139-165.

                              1 9 1 5

Leuba, James H.   "William James and Immortality," **The Journal of Philosophy,** XII (July 22), 409-416.

Porterfield, Allen Wilson.   "Lessing and Wackenroder as Anticipators of William James," **Modern Language Notes,** XXX (December), 263-264.

                              1 9 1 6

Angell, James R.   "A Reconsideration of James's Theory of Emotion in the Light of Recent Criticisms," **The Psychological Review,** XXIII (July 6), 382-383.

Sabin, Ethel E.   "James's Later View of Consciousness and the Pragmatic View: A Contrast" (Abstract), **The Journal of Philosophy,** XIII (July 6), 382-383.

                              1 9 1 7

Lowenberg, Jacob.   "The James-Lange Theory in Lessing," **The American Journal of Psychology,** XXVIII (April), 301.

                              1 9 2 1

Brett, George Sidney. **A History of Psychology,** vol. III. London: George Allen & Unwin. (Abridged and revised edition, **Brett's History of Psychology,** R. S. Peters, ed. London: George, Allen & Unwin, 1962).)

Dana, Charles L.   "The Anatomic Seat of the Emotions: A Discussion of the James-Lange Theory," **Archives of Neurology and Psychiatry,** VI, 634-639.

1 9 2 4

Baudouin, Charles. "William James's 'Talks to Teachers on Psychology'"
Contemporary Studies, translated by Eden and Ceder Paul. London:
George Allen & Unwin.

1 9 2 5

Bush, Wendell T. "William James and Panpsychism" in Studies in the History
of Ideas, vol. II. New York: Columbia University Press.

Wahl, Jean. Pluralistic Philosophies of England and America. Fred
Rothwell, trans. London: Open Court, 1925.

Wechsler, David. "What Constitutes an Emotion?" The Psychological Review,
XXXII (May), 235-240.

1 9 2 7

Cannon, Walter B. "The James-Lange Theory of Emotion: A Critical Examination and an Alternative Theory," the American Journal of Psychology,
XXXIX (December), 106-124.

Marston, William M. "Motor Consciousness as a Basis for Emotion,"Journal
of Abnormal and Social Psychology, XXII (July-September), 140-150.

1 9 2 8

Cattell, James M., "Early Psychological Laboratories," Science, 67, 543-8.

Reymert, Martin L., ed. Feelings and Emotions: The Wittenberg Symposium.
Worchester, Mass.: Clark University Press.

1 9 2 9

Boring, Edwin G. A History of Experimental Psychology. New York: The
Central Co. (Revised edition, 1950).

Cannon, Walter B. Bodily Changes in Pain, Hunger, Fear and Rage. 2nd
edition. New York: D. Appleton.

Le Breton, Maurice. **La Personalite de William James.** Paris: Hatchette, 1929.

Murphy, Gardner. **An Historical Introduction to Modern** Psychology. New York: Harcourt, Brace. (Revised edition, 1949).

1 9 3 0

Calkins, Mary Whiton. "Mary Whiton Calkins." In **A History of Psychology in Autobiography.** Volume I. Edited by Carl Murchison. Worcester, Mass.: Clark University Press, 1930, pp. 31-62.

1 9 3 2

Fernberger, Samuel W. "The American Psychological Association: A Historical Summary, 1892-1930," **Psychological Bulletin,** 29, 1-89.

Morris, Charles W.   **Six Theories of Mind.** Chicago: The University of Chicago Press.

1 9 3 3

Baum, Maurice. "The Development of James's Pragmatism Prior to 1879." **Journal of Philosophy,** 30, 43-51.

Cornesse, Marie. **Le Rôle des images dans la pensée de William James.** Grenoble: Allier pere et fils.

Heidbreder, Edna. **Seven Psychologies.** New York: Appleton-Century-Crofts.

1934

Somerville, John. "The Strange Case of Modern Psychology," **The Journal of Psychology,** XXXI (October 11), 571-577.

Townsend, Harvey Gates. **Philosophical Ideas in the United States.** New York: American Book Co.

1 9 3 5

Baum, Maurice. "William James and Psychical Research," **The Journal of Abnormal and Social Psychology,** XXX (April-June), 111-118.

Perry, Ralph Barton. The Thought and Character of William James. 2 vols. Boston: Little, Brown.

1 9 3 6

Kraushaar, Otto F. "Lotze's Influence on the Psychology of William James," The Psychological Review, XLIII (May), 235-257.

Lapan, Arthur. The Significance of James' Essay. New York: Law Printing Co.

Marhenke, Paul. "The Constituents of Mind," University of California Publications in Philosophy, XIX, 171-208.

1 9 3 8

Kraushaar, Otto F. "What James's Philosophical Orientation Owed to Lotze," The Philosophical Review XLVII (September) 517-526.

1 9 3 9

Fay, Jay Wharton. American Psychology before William James, New Brunswick, New Jersey: Rutgers University Press.

Kraushaar, Otto F. "Lotze as a Factor in the Development of James's Radical Empiricism and Pluralism," The Philosophical Review, XLVIII (September), 455-471.

1 9 4 0

Dewey, John. "The Vanishing Subject in the Psychology of James," The Journal of Philosophy, XXXVII (October 24), 589-599. Reprinted in Problems of Men. New York: Philosophical Library.

Kraushaar, Otto F. "Lotze's Influence on the Pragmatism and Practical Philosophy of William James," Journal of the History of Ideas, I (October), 439-458.

1 9 4 1

Lowe, Victor. "William James and Whitehead's Doctrine of Prehensions," The Journal of Philosophy, XXXVIII (February 27), 113-126.

Schutz, Alfred. "William James' Concept of the Stream of Thought Phenomenologically Interpreted," Philosophy and Phenomenological Research, I (June), 442-452. Reprinted in Collected Papers, vol. III. (The Hague: Nijhoff, 1966).

1 9 4 2

Blanshard, Brand and Schneider, Herbert W., eds. In Commemoration of William James: 1842-1942. New York: Columbia University Press.

Boring, Edwin G. "Human Nature vs. Sensation: William James and the Psychology of the Present," The American Journal of Psychology, LV (July), 310-327.

Brett, George Sidney. "The Psychology of William James in Relation to Philosophy" in In Commemoration of William James: 1842-1942. Abstract in The Journal of Philosophy, XXXVIII (December 4, 1941), 673.

Brotherston, Bruce W. "The Wider Setting of 'Felt Transition,'" The Journal of Philosophy, XXXIX (February 12), 97-104.

Buckham, John Wright. "William James, 1842-1942," The Personalist, XXIII (Spring), 130-149.

Cameron, Norman. "William James and Psychoanalysis" in William James: The Man and the Thinker.

Dewey, John. "William James as Empiricist" in In Commemoration of William James: 1842-1942.

Ewer, Bernard C. "The Influence of William James upon Psychology," The Personalist, XXIII (Spring), 150-158.

Holt, Edwin B. "William James as Psychologist" in In Commemoration of William James: 1842-1942.

Kantor, Jacob R. "Jamesian Psychology and the Stream of Psychological Thought" in In Commemoration of William James: 1842-1942.

Otto, Max C., and others. William James: The Man and the Thinker. Madison: University of Wisconsin Press.

Spoerl, Howard Davis. "Abnormal and Social Psychology in the Life and Work of William James," The Journal of Abnormal and Social Psychology, XXXVII (January), 3-19.

Wiggins, Forrest Oran. "William James and John Dewey," The Personalist, XXIII (Spring), 182-198.

1 9 4 3

Allport, Gordon W. "The Productive Paradoxes of William James," The Psychological Review, L (January), 95-120. Reprinted in The Person in Psychology. (Boston: Beacon Press, 1968).

Bentley, Arthur F. "The Jamesian Datum," Journal of Psychology, XVI (July), 35-79. Reprinted in Arthur F. Bentley, Inquiry into Inquiries, edited by Sidney Ratner (Boston: The Beacon Press, 1968).)

_____. "Truth, Reality, and Behavioral Fact," The Journal of Philosophy, XL (April 1), 169-187.

Gurwitsch, Aron. "William James' Theory of the 'Transitive Parts' of the Stream of Consciousness," Philosophy and Phenomenologial Research, III (June), 449-477. Reprinted in Studies in Phenomenology and Psychology (Evanston, Ill.: Northwestern University Press, 1966).

Otto, Max C. "On a Certain Blindness in William James," Ethics, LIII, 184-191.

Perry, Ralph Barton. "James the Psychologist - As a Philosopher Sees Him," The Psychologial Review, L (January), 122-124.

Pillsbury, W. B. "Titchner and James," The Psychological Review, L (January), 71-73.

Thorndike, Edward L. "James' Influence on the Psychology of Perception and Thought," The Psychological Review, L (January), 87-94.

1 9 4 5

Schutz, Alfred. "On Multiple Realities," **Philosophy and Phenomenological Research**, 5, 533-576. Reprinted in Alfred Schutz, **Collected Papers**, I, edited by Maurice Natanson. (The Hague: Martinus Nijhoff, 207-259).

1 9 4 6

Schneider, Herbert W. **A History of American Philosophy**. New York: Columbia University Press.

1 9 4 7

Gurwitsch, Aron. "On the Object of Thought," **Philosophy and Phenomenological Research**, vol. VII (1947), pp. 347-56.

1 9 4 8

Boring, Edwin G. "Masters and Pupils among the American Psychologists," **American Journal of Psychology**, 61, 527-43.

Perry, Ralph Barton. Introduction to William James's **Psychology: The Briefer Course**. Cleveland: World Publishing Company.

1 9 4 9

Harper, Robert S. "The Laboratory of William James," **Harvard Alumni Bulletin** LII (November 5), 169-173.

Lowe, Victor. "The Influence of Bergson, James, and Alexander on Whitehead," **Journal of the History of Ideas**, 10, 267-96.

Wiener, Philip P. **Evolution and the Founders of Pragmatism**. Cambridge, Mass.: Harvard University Press.

1 9 5 0

Capek, Milic. "Stream of Consciousness and 'Duree Reelle,'" **Philosophy and Phenomenological Research**, X (March), 331-353.

Harper, Robert S. "The First Psychological Laboratory," **Isis,** XLI (July) 158-161.

1 9 5 1

Jost, Josef. **Die James-Langesche Gefuhlstheorie und ihre Auswirkungen:** unter Besonderer Berucksichtigung der **"Principles"** von James. Zurich Kommerzdruk und Verlags AG.

1 9 5 2

Roback, A. A. **History of American Psychology.** New York: Library Publishers.

Capek, Milic. "The Reappearance of the Self in the Last Philosophy of William James," **The Philosophical Review,** LXII (October), 526-544.

Dennis, Wayne, and Boring, Edwin G., "The Founding of the A. P. A.," **American Psychologist,** 6, 95-7.

Isham, Chapman. "William James and the Ego Problem," **American Journal of Psychotherapy,** VII, 217-224.

Knight, Margaret. "The Permanent Contribution of William James to Psychology," **British Journal of Educational Psychology,** XXIII, 77-86.

Shouse, J. B. "David Hume and William James: a Comparison," **Journal of the History of Ideas,** 13, 514-527.

Ten, Sing-Nam. "Has James Answered Hume?" **Journal of Philosophy,** 49, 160.

1 9 5 4

Capek, Milic. "James's Early Criticism of the Automaton Theory," **Journal of the History of Ideas,** XV (April), 260-279.

Fernberger, Samuel W. "The Prestige and Impact of Various Psychologists on Psychology in America." **American Journal of Psychology,** 67, 288-98.

Madden, Edward H. "Wright, James, and Radical Empiricism," **The Journal of Philosophy,** LI (December 23), 868-874.

1 9 5 5

Hamlyn, D. M. "The Stream of Thought," **Proceedings of the Aristotelian Society,** LVI, 63-82.

1 9 5 7

Compton, Charles Herrick. **William James, Philosopher and Man.** New York: Scarecrow Press.

Gurwitsch, Aron. **Theorie du champ de la conscience.** trans. Michel Butor. Paris: Desclee de Brouwer. English original, **The Field of Consciousness** (Pittsburgh: Duquesne University Press, 1964).

1 9 5 8

Rosenzweig, Saul. "The Jameses' Stream of Consciousness," **Contemporary Psychology,** III, 250-257.

1 9 5 9

Bixler, Julius Seelye. "The Existentialists and William James," **The American Scholar,** XXVIII (Winter), 80-90.

Schmidt, Hermann. **Der Begriff der Erfahrungskontinuität bei William James und seine Bedeutung für den amerikanischen Pragmatismus.** Heidelberg: Carl Winter. (Supplementary volume to the **Jahrbuch für Amerikastudien**).

1 9 6 0

Clive, Geoffrey. **The Romantic Enlightenment.** New York: Meridan Books.

Lasswell, Harold D. "Approaches to Human Personality: William James and Sigmund Freud," **Psychoanalytic Review,** XLVII (Fall), 52-68.

Murphy, Gardner and Ballou, Roberto O., eds. **William James on Psychical Research.** New York: The Viking Press.

Smith, John E. **Themes in American Philosophy.** Purpose, Experience, and Community. New York: Harper Torchbooks.

Spiegelberg, Herbert. **The Phenomenologial Movement: A Historical Intro-duction.** The Hague: Martinus Nijhoff.

1 9 6 1

Allport, Gordon. Introduction to William James, **Psychology: The Briefer Course,** New York: Harper Torchbooks.

Stout, Cushing. "The Unfinished Arch: William James and the Idea of History," **American Quarterly,** 13, 506-515.

1 9 6 3

Martland, Thomas R. **William James and John Dewey: Process and Structure in Philosophy and Religion.** New York: Philosophical Library.

1 9 6 4

Fisch, Max H. "Philosophical Clubs in Cambridge and Boston," **Coranto,** II, 12-33, 12-25, 16-29.

Wild, John D. "William James and Existential Authenticity," **Journal of Existentialism,** 5 (1964-65), 243-256.

1 9 6 5

Edie, James M. "Note on the Philosophical Anthropology of William James" in **An Invitation to Phenomenology.** Edited by James M. Edie. Chicago: Quadrangle Books.

Rather, L. J. "Old and New Views of the Emotions and Bodily Changes: Wright and Harvey versus Descartes, James and Cannon," **Clio Medica,** I (November), 1-25.

Smith, John E. "Purpose in American Philosophy: I," **International Philosophical Quarterly,** I, #3, 390-406.

Smith, John E. "Radical Empiricism," **Proceedings of the Aristotelian Society,** NS LXV, 205-218.

Stern, Sheldon N. "William James and the New Psychology," in **Social Scien-ces at Harvard, 1860-1920,** Paul Buck, ed., Cambridge, Mass.: Harvard University Press.

1 9 6 6

Allport, Gordon W. "William James anmd the Behavioral Sciences," **Journal of the History of the Behavioral Sciences,** II (April), 145-147.

Fairbanks, Matthew. "Wittgenstein and James," **New Scholasticism,** Vol. 40, 331-340.

1 9 6 7

Allen, Gay Wilson. **William James, A Biography.** New York: Viking Press.

Beard, Robert W. "William James and the Rationality of Determinism," **Journal of the History of Philosophy,** 5, 149-156.

_____. "James's Notion of Rationality," **Darshana International,** 6, 6-12.

Boring, Edwin G. "Psychologists' Letters and Papers," **Isis,** LVIII (Spring), 103-107.

Farre, Luis. **Unamuno, William James Y Kierkegaard y otros ensayos.** Buenos Aires: Editorial La Aurora.

Reck, Andrew J. **Introduction to William James.** Bloomington: Indiana University Press, 1967.

Simon, Robert I. "Great Paths Cross: Freud and James at Clark University, 1909," **American Journal of Psychiatry,** CXXIV (December), 831-834.

1 9 6 8

Brennan, Bernard P. **William James.** New York: Twayne Publishing Co.

Conkin, Paul K. **Puritans and Pragmatists: Eight Eminent American Thinkers.** New York: Dodd, Mead.

Edie, James M. "William James and the Phenomenology of Religious Experience" in M. Novak, ed., **American Philosophy and the Future.**

Erikson, Erik H. **Identity: Youth and Crisis.** New York: W. W. Norton.

Fishman, Stephen M. "James and Lewes on Unconscious Judgement," **Journal of the History of the Behavioral Sciences,** IV (October), 335-348.

Gobar, Ash. "History of the Phenomenological Trend in the Philosophy and Psychology of William James (1942-1910)," **American Philosophical Society Yearbook,** 582-583.

Goldstein, Melvin L. "Physiological Theories of Emotion: A Critical Historical Review from the Standpoint of Behavior Theory," **Psychologial Bulletin,** LXIX (January), 23-40.

Gray, Philip Howard. "Prerequisites to an Analysis of Behaviorism: The Conscious Automaton Theory from Spaulding to William James," **Journal of the History of the Behavioral Sciences,** IV (October), 365-376.

Linschoten, Johannes. **On the Way toward a Phenomenological Psychology: The Psychology of William James.** Edited by Amedeo Giorgi. Pittsburgh: Duquesne University Press. Translated from the Dutch (Utrecht, 1959).

Marx, Otto M. "American Psychiatry without William James," **Bulletin of the History of Medicine,** XLII (January-February), 52-61.

Murphy, Murray G. "Kant's Children: The Cambridge Pragmatists," **Transactions of the Charles S. Peirce Society,** IV (Winter), 3-33.

Petras, John W. "Psychological Antecedents of Sociological Theory in America: William James and James Mark Baldwin," **Journal of the History of the Behavioral Sciences,** IV (April), 132-142.

Rosenzweig, Saul. "William James and the Stream of Thought" in **Historical Roots of Contemporary Psychology.** Edited by B. B. Wolman. New York: Harper and Row. French translation, "William James et le courant de conscience," **Bulletin de Psychologie,** XXIII (1969-1970), 1001-1009.

Shields, Allan. "On a Certain Blindness in William James and Others," **Journal of Aesthetics and Art Criticism,** 27, 27-34.

Smith, John E. "William James as Philosophical Psychologist," Midway, VIII (Winter), 3-19.

Strout, Cushing. "Ego Psychology and the Historian," History and Theory, VII, 281-297.

_____. "William James and the Twice-Born Sick Soul," Daedalus, XCVII

(Summer), 1062-1082.

_____. "The Pluralistic Identity of William James: A Psychological Reading of The Varieties of Religious Experience," American Quarterly, 23, 134-52.

Thayer, H. S. Meaning and Action: A Critical History of Pragmatism. Indianapolis: Bobbs-Merrill.

Wilshire, Bruce. William James and Phenomenology: A Study of 'The Principles of Psychology.' Bloomington: Indiana University Press.

1 9 6 9

Dilworth, D. "The Initial Formulations of 'Pure Experience' in Nishida Kitaro and William James," Monumenta Nipponica, 24, 93-111.

Edie, James M. "Necessary Truth and Perception: William James on the Structure of Experience" in New Essays in Phenomenology. Edited by J. M. Edie. Chicago: Quadrangle Books.

Ehman, Robert R. "William James and the Structure of the Self" in New Essays in Phenomenology. Edited by J. M. Edie. Chicago: Quadrangle Books.

Greenlee, Douglas. Review of A. J. Ayer The Origins of Pragmatism (1968) and H. S. Thayer Meaning and Action (1968), Journal of the History of Ideas, XXX (October-December), 603-608.

Harlow, Harry F. "William James and Instinct Theory" in R. B. MacLeod, ed., William James (1969).

Hilgard, Ernest R. "Levels of Awareness: Second Thoughts on Some of William James' Ideas" in R. B. MacLeod, ed., William James (1969).

Kersten, Fred. "Franz Brentano and William James," **Journal of the History of Philosophy,** VII (April), 177-191.

Krech, David. "Does Behavior Really Need a Brain? In Praise of William James: Some Historical Musings, Vain Lamentations, and a Sounding of Great Expectations" in R. B. MacLeod, ed., **William James** (1969).

MacLeod, Robert B., ed. **William James: Unfinished Business.** Washington, D.C.: American Psychological Association.

May, Rollo. "William James' Humanism and the Problem of the Will" in R. B. MacLeod, ed., **William James** (1969).

Meyers, Robert G. "Natural Realism and Illusion in James's Radical Empiricism," **Transactions of the Charles S. Peirce Society,** V (Fall), 211-223.

Meyers, Gerald E. "William James's Theory of Emotion," **Transactions of the Charles S. Peirce Society,** V (Spring), 67-89.

Schrag, Calvin O. "Struktur der Erfahrung in der Philosophie von James und Whitehead," **Zeitschrift für philosophische Forschung,** XXIII, 479-494.

Wild, John Daniel. "William James and the Phenomenology of Belief" in **New Essays in Phenomenology.** Edited by J. M. Edie. Chicago: Quadrangle Books.

_____. **The Radical Empiricism of William James.** Garden City, N.Y.: Doubleday.

Wilshire, Bruce. "Protophenomenology in the Psychology of William James," **Transactions of the Charles S. Peirce Society,** V (Winter), 25-43.

1 9 7 0

Edie, James M. "William James and Phenomenology," **The Review of Metaphysics,** XXIII (March), 481-526.

Fehr, Fred S. and Stern, John A. "Peripheral Physiological Variables and Emotion: The James-Lange Theory Revisited," **Psychological Bulletin,** LXXIV (December), 411-424.

Feinstein, Howard M. "William James on the Emotions," **Journal of the History of Ideas,** XXXI (January-March), 133-142.

Gobar, Ash. "The Phenomenology of William James," **Proceedings of the American Philosophical Society,** CXIV (August), 294-309.

Gould, James A. "R. B. Perry on the Origin of American and European Pragmatism," **Journal of the History of Philosophy,** VIII (October), 431-450.

Kauber, Peter. "The Development of the New Pragmatic Theory of the A Priori," **Kinesis,** 3, 9-33.

Marshall, G. D. "Attention and Will," **Philosophical Quarterly,** 20, 14-25.

Rosenzweig, Saul. "Erik Erikson on William James's Dream: A Note of Correction," **Journal of the History of the Behavioral Sciences,** VI (July), 258-260.

1 9 7 1

Chamberlain, Gary L. "The Drive for Meaning in William James's Analysis of Religious Experience," **Journal of Value Inquiry,** V (Summer), 194-206.

Eisendrath, Craig R. **The Unifying Moment: The Psychological Philosophy of William James and Alfred North Whitehead.** Cambridge, Mass.: Harvard University Press.

Hale, Nathan G. **Freud and the Americans: The Beginnings of Psychoanalysis in the United States, 1876-1917.** New York: Oxford University Press.

_____. James Jackson Putnam and Psychoanalysis: Letters Between Putnam and Sigmund Freud, Ernest Jones, William James, Sandor Ferenczi, and Mortin Prince, 1877-1917. Cambridge, Mass.: Harvard University Press.

Mathur, D. C. Naturalistic Philosophies of Experience: Studies in James, Dewey and Farber Against the Background of Husserl's Phenomenology, St. Louis, Mo.: Warren H. Green.

Meyers, Robert G. "Meaning and Metaphysics in James," Philosophy and Phenomenological Research, 31, 369-380.

Murphy, Gardner. "William James on the Will," Journal of the History of the Behavioral Sciences, VII (July), 249-260.

Myers, Gerald E. "William james on Time Perception," Philosophy of Science, 38, 353-360.

Pancheri, Lillian U. "James Lewis and the Pragmatic A Priori," Transactions of the Charles S. Peirce Society, VII (Summer), 135-149.

Phillips, D. C. "James, Dewey, and the Reflex Arc," Journal of the History of Ideas, XXXII (October-December), 555-568.

Reck, Andrew J. "The Philosophical Psychology of William James," Southern Journal of Philosophy, IX (Fall), 293-312.

Spicker, Stuart F. "William James and Phenomenology," Journal of the British Society for Phenomenology, vol. II, no. 3 (October), 69-74.

Tibbetts, Paul. "William James and the Doctrine of 'Pure Experience,'" University of Dayton Review, VIII (Summer), 43-58.

_____. "The Philosophy of Science of William James: An Unexplored Dimension of James's Thought," The Personalist, LII (Summer), 535-556.

Wilshire, Bruce. "A Reply to Stuart Spicker's 'William James and Phenomenology,'" The Journal of the British Society for Phenomenology, 2, 75-80.

1972

Bergson, Henri. Melanges, edited by Andre Robinet. Paris: Presses Universitaires de France.

Cadwallader, Thomas C. and Cadwallader, Joyce V. "America's First Modern Psychologist: William james or Charles S. Peirce?", Proceedings of the 80th Annual Convention of the American Philosophical Association, Contributed Papers and Symposia, VII, 773-774.

De Aloysio, Francesco. Da Dewey a James. Roma: Bulzoni.

Johnson, Ellwood. "William James and the Art of Fiction," Journal of Aesthetics and Art Criticism, XXX (Spring), 285-296.

Reck, Andrew J. "Dualisms in William James's Principles of Psychology, Tulane Studies in Philosophy, XXI, 23-38.

Spiegelberg, Herbert. "What William James Knew about Edmund Husserl" in Life-World and Consciousness: Essays for Aron Gurwitsch. Edited by Lester E. Embree. Evanston: Ill.: Northwestern University Press.

Wertz, Spencer K. "On Wittgenstein and James." The New Scholasticism, 46, 446-448.

1 9 7 3

Carlsson, P. Allan. "Jung and James on the Typology of World Views," The Journal of General Education, XXV (July), 113-119.

Edie, James M. "The Genesis of a Phenomenological Theory of the Experience of Personal Identity: William James on Consciousness and the Self," Man and World, VI (September), 322-340.

Hook, Sidney. "William James and George Santayana," I Carb S (Southern Illinois University, Carbondale), Vol. I, No. 1 (Fall-Winter), 35-39.

Reck, Andrew J. "Epistemology in William James's Principles of Psychology, Tulane Studies in Philosophy, XXII (1973), 79-115.

1 9 7 4

Dooley, Patrick Kiaran. Pragmatism as Humanism: The Philosophy of William James. Chicago: Nelson Hall.

Gini, A. R. "Radical Subjectivism in the Thought of William James," The New Scholasticism, XLVIII (Autumn), 509-518.

Rosenthal, Sandra B. "Recent Perspectives on American Pragmatism: Part I," **Transactions of the Charles S. Peirce Society**, 10, 76-93; Part II, 166-184.

Stevens, Richard. **James and Husserl: The Foundations of Meaning. Phaenomenologica**, Vol. LX. The Hague: Nijhoff.

1 9 7 5

Bixler, J. S. "Relevance in The Philosophy of William James," **Religious Humanism**, 9 (Winter), 38-44.

Browning, Don. "William James's Philosophy of the Person: The Concept of the Strenuous Life," **Zygon**, 10 (June), 162-174.

Edie, James M. "John Wild's Interpretation of William James's Theory of the Free Act." **Man and World**, 8 (May), 136-140.

Fizer, John. "Ingarden's Pases, Bergson's **Duree Reele**, and William James's Stream: Metaphoric Variants or Mutually Exclusive Concepts on the Theme of Time," **Dialectics and Humanism**, 2 (Summer), 33-48.

Fullinwider, S. P. "William James's Spiritual Crisis," **The Historian**, 13, 39-57.

Giuffrida, Robert. "James on Meaning and Significance." **Transactions fo the Charles S. Peirce Society**, 11, 18-36.

Helm, Bertrand P. "William James on the Nature of Time," **Tulane Studies** in Philosophy, 24, 33-47.

Hocks, Richard A. **Henry James and Pragmatistic Thought: A Study in the Relationship between the Philosophy of William James and the Literary Art of Henry James.** Chapel Hill: University of North Carolina Press.

Malone, John C. "William James and B. F. Skinner: Behaviorism, Reinforcement, and Interest," **Behaviorism**, 3 (2), 140-151.

Scott, Frederick J. Down. "William James and Stanford University: 1898-1905," **San Jose Studies**, Vol. 1, 9-23, Fall.

_____. "William James and Stanford University: 1906," **San Jose Studies,** Vol. 1, 28-43.

1 9 7 6

Bayley, James E. "A Jamesian Theory of the Self." **Transactions of the Charles S. Peirce Society,** 12, 148-65.

Corti, Walter Robert, ed. **The Philosophy of William James.** Hamburg: Felix Meiner Verlag.

Cronk, George Francis. "James and the Problem of Intersubjectivity," in W. P. Corti, ed., The Philosophy of William James, 221-244.

Czerwionke, Felecia. "The Self in William James' Psychology," in W. R. Corti, ed., The Philosophy of William James, 201-220.

Daniel, Stephen J. "Fringes and Transitive States in William James' Concept of the Stream of Thought," **Auslegung,** 3 (March), 64-80.

David, Keith R. "Percept and Concept in William James," in W. R. Corti, ed., The Philosophy of William James, 133-146.

Deledalle, Gerard. "William James and his Father: A Study in Characterology," in W. R. Corti, ed., The Philosophy of William James, 317-330.

Eames, Elizabeth R. "A Pragmatic Concept of Causation," in W. R. Corti, ed. The Philosophy of William James, 119-132.

Embree, Lester. "William James and Some Problems of Idealism," **Der Idealismus** und **Seine Gegenwart,** Festschrift für Werner Marx, ed. Ute Guzzoni, Bernard Rang, and Ludwig Siep, Hamburg: Felix Meiner Verlag, pp. 101-115.

Flower, Elizabeth F. "The Unity of Knowledge and Purpose in James's View of Action," in W. R. Corti, ed., The Philosophy of William James, 179-199.

Gavin, William J. "William James and the Indeterminacy of Language and 'The Really Real,'" Proceedings of Catholic Philosophical Association, 50, 208-218.

_____. "William James on Language," International Philosophical Quarterly, 16, 81-86.

_____. "William James and the Importance of 'The Vague,'" Cultural Hermeneutics, 3, 245-265.

_____. "William James' Attitude Toward Death," Journal of Thought, 11, 199-204, July.

Lowe, Victor. "The Relation between James and Whitehead," in W. R. Corti, ed., The Philosophy of William James, 331-345.

Madden, Edward H., and Charkrabarti, Chandana. "James's 'Pure Experience' versus Ayer's 'Weak Phehomenalism.'" Transactions of the Charles S. Peirce Society, 12, 3-17.

Madden, Edward H., and Hare, Peter H., "A Critical Appraisal of James's View of Causality," in W. R. Corti, ed., The Philosophy of William James, 101-117.

McDermott, John J. "A Metaphysics of Relations: James's Anticipations of Contemporary Experience," in W. R. Corti, The Philosophy of William James, 81-99.

Miller, David L. "William James and the Specious Present," in W. R. Cordi, The Philosophy of William James, 51-79.

McDermott, John J. "A Metaphysics of Relations: James's Anticipation of Contemporary Experience," in W. R. Corti, ed., The Philosophy of William James, 81-99.

Oliver, W. Donald. "James's Cerebral Dichotomy," in W. R. Corti, ed., The Philosophy of William James, 33-49.

Ross, Robert. "William James: The Wider Consciousness," Philosophy Today, 20, 134-148.

Schneider, Herbert W. "Healthy Minds with Sick Souls," in W. R. Corti, The Philosophy of William James, 357-377.

Seigfried, Charlene Haddock. "The Structure of Experience for William James," Transactions of the Charles S. Peirce Society, 12 (Fall), 330-347.

Skousgaard, Stephen. "The Phenomenology in William James' Philosophical Psychology," Journal of the British Society for Phenomenology, 7, 86-95.

1 9 7 7

Dooley, Patrick K. "The Structure of a Science of Psychology: William James and B. F. Skinner," Philosophy in Context, Vol. 6, 54-69.

Herms, Eilert. Radical Empiricism: Studien zur Psychologie, Metaphysik und Religionstheorie William James'. 1. Aufl. Güttersloh: Güttersloher Verlaghaus Mohn.

Howells, E. G. "Hume, Shaftsburg, and the Peirce-James Philosophical Psychology," Journal of the British Society for Phenomenology, 7, 86-95.

Jubin, B. "Spatial Quale: A Corrective to James's Radical Empiricism," Journal of the History of Philosophy 15, 212-216.

Kuklick, Bruce, The Rise of American Philosophy: Cambridge, Massachusetts, 1860-1930, New Haven: Yale University Press.

Liszka, Jacob. "James's Psycho-physical Parallelism and the Question of the Self in the Principles of Psychology." Journal of Phenomenological Psychology, Vol. 8, 66-80.

McDermott, John J., ed. The Writings of William James. Chicago: University of Chicago Press.

Oppenheim, F. M. "Royce's Community: A Dimension Missing in Freud and James?" Journal of the History of the Behavioral Sciences, 13, 173-190.

Pastore, Nicholas. "William James: A Contradiction," Journal of the History of the Behavioral Sciences, 13, 126-30.

Scott, Stanley J. "Wallace Stevens and William James: The Poetics of Pure Experience," Philosophy of Literature, 1, 183-191.

Skrupskelis, Ignas K. William James: A Reference Guide, Boston: G. H. Hall, XVIII.

Thayer, H. S. "On William James on Truth," Transactions of the Charles S. Peirce Society, 13, 3-19.

Walter, Edward. "William James's Chance," Midwest Journal of Philosophy, 5, 51-59.

Wilshire, Bruce W. "William James, Phenomenology and Pragmatism: A Reply to Rosenthal," Transactions of the Charles S. Peirce Society, 13, 45-55.

1 9 7 8

High, Richard P. "Does James's Reference to Helmholtz Really Involve a Contadiction?" Journal of the History of the Behavioral Sciences, 14, 337-43.

Johanningmeier, Erwin V. "Ruminations on the Beginnings of Educational Psychology: William James and the Foundations of a Profession," Education Theory, 28, 111-119.

Madden, Marian C. "William James and the Problem of Relations," Transactions of the Charles S. Peirce Society, 14, 227-246, Fall.

Ross, Barbara. "William James: A Prime Mover in the Psychoanalytic Movement in America," in George E. Gifford, ed., Psychoanalysis and Psychotherapy and the New England Scene, New York: Science History Publications, 10-24.

Seigfried, Charlene Haddock. Chaos and Context: A Study of William James. Athens, Ohio: Ohio University Press.

Taylor, Eugene I. "Psychology of Religion and Asian Studies: the William
    James Legacy," Southern Journal of Transpersonal Psychology, 10 (1),
    67-69.

                        1 9 7 9

Embree, Lester. "The Phenomenology of Speech in the Early William James,"
    Journal of the British Society for Phenomenology, 10, pp. 101-109.

Gavin, William J. "Herzen and James: Freedom as Radical," Studies in
    Soviet Thought (Netherlands), 14, 213-229.

Madden, Edward H. "The Psychosomatic Illness of William James," Thought,
    54, 376-392.

Miller, Harcy C. "William James and Twentieth Century Ethnic Thought,"
    American Quarterly, 31, 533-55.

Reck, Andrew J. "William James on Ultimate Reality and Meaning," Ultimate
    Reality and Meaning, 2, 40-58.

_____. "Idealistic Metaphysics in William James's 'Principles of
    Psychology'" Idealistic Studies, 9, 213-221.

Tavuzzi, Michael. "A Note on Husserl's Dependence on William James,"
    Journal of the British Sociey for Phenomenology, 10. 194-196.

                        1 9 8 0

Browning, Don S. Pluralism and Personality: William James and Some Contem-
    porary Cultures of Psychology. Lewisburg, PA.: Bucknell University
    Press, 1980.

Gale, Richard M. "William James and the Ethics of Belief," American
    Philosophical Quarterly, 17, 1-14.

McDermott, John J. "The Promethean Self and Community in the Philosophy of
    William James," Rice University Studies, 66, 87-101.

MacKenzie. Lynne. "William James and the Problem of Interests," Journal
    of the History of the Behavioral Sciences, 16, 175-85.

Rambo, Lewis R. "Ethics, Evolution, and the Psychology of William James," **Journal of the History of the Behavioral Sciences,** 16, 50-7.

Rosenthal, Sandra B. & Bourgeois, Patrick L. **Pragmatism and Phenomenology.** Amsterdam: B. R. Gruner.

Sessions, William L. "William James and the Right to Over-Believe," **Philosophy Research Archives,** 7, 1420.

Sprigge, T. L. S. "The Distinctiveness of American Philosophy," in Caws, Peter, ed., **Two Centuries of Philosophy in America,** Totowa, NJ: Roman & Littlefield, XVII.

Woodward, William R., "William James and Gordon Allport: Parallels in their Maturing Conceptions of Self and Personality," in **Psychology: Historical and Theoretical Perspectives,** New York: Academic Press.

1 9 8 1

Aiken, Henry D. "William James as Moral and Social Philosopher," **Philosophic Exchange,** 3, 55-69.

Arms, George. "Some Varieties of Howells' Religious Experience," in Girgus, Sam B., ed., **The American Self: Myth, Ideology, and Religion.** Alburquerque: University of New Mexico Press.

Campbell, James. "William James and the Ethics of Fulfillment," **Transactions fo the Charles S. Peirce Society,** 17, 224-240.

Ford, Marcus P. "William James: Positiviste, Phenomenologue ou Pragmatiste?" **Archives de Philosophie** 44, 455-477.

Georgi, Amedeo. "On the Relationships among the Psychologist's Fallacy, Psychologism, and the Phenomenological Reduction," **Journal of Phenomenological Psychology,** 12, 75-86.

Hart, Joseph. "The Significance of William James' Ideas for Modern Psychotherapy," **Journal of Contemporary Psychotherapy,** 12 (2) 88-102.

High, Richard P. "Shadworth Hodgson and William James's Formulation of Space Perception: Phenomenology and Perceptual Realism," **Journal of the History of the Behavioral Sciences,** 17, 466-85.

Levinson, Henry S. The **Religious Investigations of William James.** Chapel Hill: University of North Carolina Press.

Pastore, Nicholas. "Dr. High on History." **Journal of the History of the Behavioral Sciences,** 17, 486-9.

Ruddick, Lisa. "Fluid Symbols in American Modernism: William James, Gurtrude Stein, Ayana, and Wallace Stevens," in Bloomfield, Morton W., ed., **Allegory, Myth and Symbol,** Cambridge: Harvard University Press.

Seigfried, Charlene Haddock. "James's Reconstruction of Ordinary Experience," Southern Journal of Philosophy 19, 499-516.

Schoenewolf, Caroll. "Jamesian Psychology and Nathaniel West's **Miss Lonelyhearts.**" San Jose Studies, 7 (3): 80-86.

Slone, Douglas. "William James as an Educator," in **Education and Values,** New York: Teachers College Press, Colombia University.

Sprigge, T. L. S. "James, Santayana, Tarski, and Pragmatism," in **Pragmatism and Purpose:** Essays Presented to Thomas A. Goudge, L. W. Summer editor, (Toronto: University of Toronto Press) pp. 105-120.

Summersgill, Harue. "The Influence of William James and Henri Bergson on Natsume Soseki's Hiugan Sugi Madem," **Kyushu American Literature,** Fukuoka 810, Japan.

1 9 8 2

Brinton, A. "William James and the Epistemic View of Rhetoric," **Quarterly Journal of Speech** 69, 158-69.

DeArmey, Michael H. "William James and the Problem of Other Minds," Southern Journal of Philosophy, 20, 325-336.

Dooley, Patrick K. "Fakes and Good Frauds: Pragmatic Religion in the Damnation of Theron Ware," **American Lituraturary Realism,** 1870-1910, Arlington, Texas, 15 (1), 74-85.

Ford, Marcus Peter. **William James's Philosophy: A New Perspective,** Amherst: University of Massachusetts Press.

High, Richard P. "Dr. High on Dr. Pastore on 'Dr. High on History': James's Theory of Space Perception," **Journal of the History of the Behavioral Sciences,"** 18, 176-80.

McNulty, Michael T. "James, Mach and the Problem of Other Minds," **Transactions of the Charles S. Peirce Society,** 18, 244-254.

Michaels, Walter B. "Getting Physical," **Raritan: A Quarterly Review,** New Brunswick, NJ, 2 (2): 103-113.

Robinson, Daniel N. **Toward a Science of Human Nature: Essays on the Psychologies of Mill, Hegel, Wundt and James,** New York: Columbia University Press.

Ruccick, Lisa. "Melanctha and the Psychology of William James," **Modern Fiction Studies,** Winter, 28 (4): 545-556.

Seigfried, Charlene Haddock. "Vagueness and the Adequacy of Concepts," **Philosophy** Today, 26, 357-67.

Stevens, Richard Cobb. "A Fresh Look at James's Radical Empiricism," in **Phenomenology, Dialogues and Bridges,** Ronald Bruzina, editor, Albany: State University of New York Press, pp. 109-121.

Suckiel, Ellen Kappy. **The Pragmatic Philosophy of William James,** Notre Dame University Press.

Tintner, Adeline R. "Henry and William James and Titian's Torn Glove," **IRIS: Notes in the History of Art,** 1: 22-24.

1983

Bjork, Daniel W. **The Compromised Scientist: William James in the Development of American Psychology.** New York: Columbia University Press.

Boren, L. S. "William James, Theodore Dreiser and the Anaesthetic Revolution," **American Studies,** 24, 5-17.

Field, Richard W. "William James and the Epochal Theory of Time," **Process Studies,** 13, 260-274.

Scott, Frederick J. D. "William James and the Concord School of Philosophy," **San Jose Studies**, 9, 34-40.

Seigfried, Charlene Haddock. "The Philosopher's 'License': William James and Common Sense," **Transactions of the Charles S. Peirce Society,** 19, 273-290.

Wagner, Helmuth R. **Phenomenology of Consciousness and Sociology of the Life-World: An Introduction,** Edmunton, Alberta, Canada: University of Alberta Press.

1 9 8 4

Feinstein, Howard M. **Becoming William James,** Ithaca and London: Cornell University Press.

Morrow, Felix. "William James and John Dewey on Consciousness: Suppressed Writings," **Journal of Humanistic Psychology,** 24 (Winter), 69-79.

Reck, Andrew. "The Influence of William James on John Dewey in Psychology," **Transactions of the Charles S. Peirce Society,** 20 (Spring), 87-117.

Seigfried, Charlene Haddock. "The Positivist Foundation of William James's Principles," **The Review of Metaphysics,** 37 (March), 579-593.

Wilson, Daniel J. "Neurasthenia and Vocational Crisis in Post-Civil War America," **Psychohistorical Review,** 12 (Spring), 3108.

American Dissertations on James's Psychology

1 9 1 3

Patterson, Herbert Parsons. **An Extension of the Pure Experience Philosophy of William James,** Yale University.

1 9 2 7

Long, W. H. **The Philosophy of Charles Renouvier and its Influence on William James,** Harvard University.

Rosenberger, H. E. **An Appraisal of the Ethics of William James,** Yale University.

1 9 2 8

Baum, Maurice James. **Genetic Study of the Philosophies of William James and John Dewey,** University of Chicago.

1 9 3 3

Province, Robert Calhoun. **The Voluntarism of William James: An Historical and Critical Study,** Brown University.

1 9 4 9

MacMillan, Donald. **William James's Philosophy of Religion, with Specific Reference to his Philosophy of Mind,** University of Toronto.

1 9 5 3

Kunz, Robert M. **A Critical Examination of the Radical Empiricism of William James,** State University of New York at Buffalo.

1 9 6 0

Koller, Alice Ruth. **The Concept of Emotion: A Study of the Analyses of James, Russell, and Ryle,** Radcliffe College.

1 9 6 3

Bluestone, Natalie Suzanne Harris. **Time and Consciousness in Jean-Paul Sartre and William James,** Johns Hopkins University.

Manicas, Peter Theodore. **The Concept of the Individual in the Philosophies of William Graham Sumner, William James, Josiah Royce, and Lester Ward,** State University of New York at Buffalo.

1 9 6 5

Matthews, William. **An Evaluation of the Radical Empiricism of William James and its Theological Significance for the Problem of Identity,** University of Chicago.

1 9 6 6

Charron, William Cletus. **An Exposition and Analysis of William James's Views** on the Nature of Man, Marquette University.

Platt, Thomas Walter. **Spencer and James on Mental Categories: A Reevaluation** in Light of Modern Biology, University of Pennsylvania.

Wilshire, Bruce Withington. **Natural Science** and **Phenomenology: William** James's "Principles of Psychology" as a Search for Reconciliation, New York University.

1 9 6 9

Bayley, James E. **Self and Personal Identity in William James's "Principles of Psychology"**, Columbia University.

David, Keith Raymond. **Percept and Concept in William James,** Southern Illinois University.

Dooley, Patrick Kiaran. **Humanism in the Philosophy of William James,** University of Notre Dame.

Earle, William James. **James's Stream of Thought as Point of Departure for Metaphysics,** Columbia University.

Todd, Quintin Robert. **James, Whitehead, and Radical Empiricism,** Pennsylvania State University.

1 9 7 0

Corello, Anthony V. **Structure of the Field of Consciousness: A Study of Part-Whole Organization in William James's** Epistemology, New School for Social Research.

Marshall, Ernest Clare. **An Explication of William James' Neutral Monism and Some Applications to his Pragmatism,** Ohio State University.

Nisula, Einer Salo. **Thought and Action in William James,** Michigan State University.

1972

Visgak, Charles Anthrony. **The Physiological Theory of the Emotions as the Foundation for the Moral Judgment of the Individual According to William James**, Duquesne University.

1973

Cwi, David. **William James's "Pure Experience" Philosophy: Genesis and Criticism**, Johns Hopkins University.

DeLoach, William. **The Vocation of William James: An Essay in Literary Biography**, University of Illinois, Urbana-Champaign.

Seigfried, Charlene Haddock. **The Status of Relations in William James**, Loyola University of Chicago.

Wagenaar, John. **Behaviorism and Religous Experience: An Investigation of B. F. Skinner Through William James**, University of Chicago.

1974

Czerwionka, Felicia Emily. **The Self in William James's Psychology**, University of Notre Dame.

1975

Kirkpatrick, Judith Ann. **The Artistic Expression of the Psychological Theories of William James in the Writings of Henry James**, University of Delaware.

Rambo, Lewis R. **The Strenuous Life: William James's Normative Vision of the Human**, University of Chicago.

1976

Borton, Robert Leroy. **The Relation between Pluralism and Pragmatism in the Philsophy of William James**, Claremont Graduate School.

Giuffrida, Robert Thomas, Jr. **Chauncy Wright and William James on Significance and the Concept of the Given**, State University of New York at Buffalo.

1 9 7 7

Feinstein, Howard Marvin. **Fathers and Sons: Work and the Inner World of William James, an Intergenerational Inquiry**, Cornell University.

Knox, Amie Bushman. **An Approach to Education Emanating from William James and Alfred Schutz**, Columbia University Teachers College.

1 9 7 8

DeArmey, Michael Howard. **The Philosophical Anthropology of William James: Towards a Complete Teleological Analysis of the Nature, Origin, and Destiny of Human Beings.** Tulane University.

High, Richard Paul. **Shadworth Hodgson and the Psychology of William James: Experience, Teleology and Realism**, University of New Hampshire.

Marr, David Marshall. **"The Infinitude of the Private Man": Essays on Emerson, Whitman, William James, Blackmur, and Heller**, Washington State University.

1 9 7 9

Laguardia, David M. **Advance on Chaos: Varieties of Imagination in Emerson, William James and Wallace Stevens**, Kent State University.

1 9 8 0

Bock, Layeh Aronson. **The Birth of Modernism: "Des Imagistes" and the Psychology of William James**, Stanford University.

Caste, Nicholas Joseph. **The Mind-Body Relation in the Philosophy of William James**, Emory University.

Davidove, Douglas Martin. **Theories of Introjection and Their Relation to William James's Concept of Belief: An Application of the Unitary Approacha of Gestalt Therapy**, New York University.

Seeman, Herbert A. **William James's Model of Organic Idealism**, Washington State University.

1 9 8 2

Pruitt, Richard Gerald. **William James's Intentions: Concepts, Truth, and Value,** Boston University.

Ruddick, Lisa Cole. **Models of Consciousness in the Works of William James, Gertrude Stein and George Santayana,** Harvard University.

1 9 8 3

Frett, Peter Bernard. **Pragmatism and Education: A Study of William James and George Herbert Mead's Models of Self-Genesis,** The University of Chicago.

Mazoue, James. **The Conceptual Translation of the Perceptual Flux in the Philosophy of William James,** Tulane University.

1 9 8 4

O'Briant, Mary Prevette. **William James: "The Principles of Psychology" Reconsidered,** University of Georgia.

Glover, Roy Arvid. **Josiah Royce and William James: Philosophers of the Community and the Individual,** University of Minnesota.

McFadden, Mark Gerald. **On the Periphery of the Absolute: William James's Critique of British Hegelianism,** University of California, Berkeley.

INDEX OF NAMES

INDEX OF TOPICS